Pearce M.
North

THE ACCOUNTABILITY
CONNECTION

THE
ACCOUNTABILITY
CONNECTION

Matt Friedeman

VICTOR BOOKS®

A DIVISION OF SCRIPTURE PRESS PUBLICATIONS INC.
USA CANADA ENGLAND

Unless otherwise noted, Scripture quotations are from the *Holy Bible, New International Version,* © 1973, 1978, 1984, International Bible Society. Used by permission of Zondervan Bible Publishers; other quotations are from the *New American Standard Bible* (NASB), © the Lockman Foundation 1960, 1962, 1963, 1968, 1971, 1972, 1973, 1975, 1977; *The New King James Version* (NKJV), © 1979, 1980, 1982, Thomas Nelson, Inc., Publishers; J.B. Phillips: *The New Testament in Modern English* (PH), Revised Edition, © J.B. Phillips, 1958, 1960, 1972, permission of Macmillan Publishing Co. and Collins Publishers.

Copyediting: Ben Unseth, Barbara Williams
Cover Design: Scott Rattray

Library of Congress Cataloging-in-Publication Data

Friedeman, Matt.
    The accountability connection / by Matt Friedeman.
        p.   cm.
    Includes bibliographical references.
    ISBN 0-89693-052-1
    1. Christian life—1960-   I. Title.
BV4501.2.F7625   1992
248.4—dc20   91-30585
                                              CIP

1 2 3 4 5 6 7 8 9 10 Printing/Year 96 95 94 93 92

To my sister Lisa.

She excited me about Jesus,
continues to disciple me with her terrific and enthusiastic
   example,
and is a source of inspiration as she invests her life into the
   people of this world that matter most – her family.

ACKNOWLEDGMENTS

Thanks to Ray Easley, Bill Ury, and Susan Arnold for reading, encouraging, correcting, and generally providing good accountability for me in this project.

Tim Wright, who has traveled through several classes with me, deserves much credit for his helpful suggestions and also for his input on the Bible study section. In this effort he has turned out to be not only a good student but a good teacher as well. Marlin Betts also handed along some suggestions and for these I am grateful.

And, of course, appreciation to my wife Mary whose writing, thinking skills, and patience far exceed mine. I love you.

CONTENTS

Bulletin Board

Accountability — the state of being held liable or responsible; to give account for the thinking, feeling, and actions of a person.

Small Group Accountability — giving others permission, in a group of 2–6 people, to hold you responsible for agreed upon group objectives and/or objectives you set for yourself. The Christian accountability group tries, in the power of God's Spirit, to develop Christlike living, character, service, and community.

PREFACE

The thought struck me with force one day. At every point in our society where we demand excellence, we implement intense accountability.

Think about it. Most athletic teams have extensive systems of accountability. The coach teaches, the athlete performs, the coach refines, the athlete adjusts and tries again, and the cycle goes on. In practice, in games, even in whole seasons, the players, coaches, and teams that carry out instructions excel and are rewarded. Those who don't follow these simple rules are certainly held accountable — they get with the program or get off the team. It may sound harsh, but you and I know that is how excellence in athletics happens. Accountability is necessary in sport.

The working American knows about accountability. Show up for work on time, master your tasks exceptionally well, get along with your workmates and boss — and you get more money, a better position, an opportunity to climb the ladder. Become lax in any of the above, and you are demoted in position and pay. People are watching. And we expect them to. We recognize accountability as normal in the working world. Accountability is necessary for profitable businesses.

My students dream of the day when I might walk into class, throw the syllabus in the trash can, and announce, "Class, forget assignments, forget the tests, forget the attendance requirements, forget grades. Let's just do what we're supposed to do in class — learn!" I doubt the structure, or rather the lack of it, would have a desirable educational effect. Little learning would take place in an environment void of significant accountability. I give guidelines and rules to live by, and the students interested in an education need them. Accountability is necessary for education.

Walk into my church on a Sunday morning and wait for announcement time. Usually at least one person, frequently more, announces a sobriety birthday, marking one, or eight, or twenty addiction-free years. We all applaud, whistle, laugh a little, sing "Happy Birthday," and then continue with the rest of the service. It is a happy time. But nobody ever asks the question, "How'd you do it?" Everybody knows. These people recognized a desperate need in their lives and went to a Twelve-step program like Alcoholics Anonymous. They took accountability, confession, support, and most of all, change seriously. And they licked their addictions. And we know, beyond the shadow of a doubt, that accountability made the victory possible. Accountability is necessary for healing.

Speaking of addictions, my problem happens to be overeating. And guess what—when I finally gathered that I had a weight problem, where did I go but to a club of people who placed me on a reasonable diet, provided plenty of group encouragement, and forced me on to a scale once a week. I lost weight. All the group members lost weight. And accountability was the key.

In all things we deem important, everywhere we demand excellence, we see accountability. It doesn't matter whether it is athletics or business, medicine or politics, academics or addiction—relationships that are caring yet constructive are the key to excellence, achievement, and recovery.

Question: Why do we tend to shun spiritual accountability? In this most important dimension of our lives, why do we avoid accountability to fellow believers in Christ? Is it because of the abuses we may have heard of? Or because we consider religious experience a private affair? Or because of a lack of examples? Probably all of the above are factors, and we will address them later. But the fundamental answer lies elsewhere.

Sociological research indicates that the Western world has departed from a basic framework of community. Whether church, family, or neighborhoods, we have moved from interdependence to independence, from team to individual, from working together to pulling apart. Some analysts call it the "Me" generation; the Christian would say that we have departed from an essential reflection of the image of God—an idea we will pick up on in chapter 1.

But across the nation and world today small pockets of Christians gather on a regular basis to stimulate one another to victorious living and to "press on toward the goal" (Phil. 3:14) in Christ Jesus. Healthy accountability groups are refreshing, motivating, searching, convicting, but always, always, focused on Jesus as Savior and Lord, and the Holy Spirit as an empowering, cleansing, teaching Presence. This volume is written for those interested in, or curious about, such a group experience.

In this handbook I have tried to do three things:
• give the reader a brief biblical, historical, and practical foundation for the use of small group accountability (chap. 1).
• investigate seven different areas of our lives on which we should focus as we seek to be all we were meant to be in Christ Jesus. Areas covered include: the devotional life, mission, money, sex, health, family, daily Christian living (chaps. 2–8).
• provide the reader with some practical guidelines for implementing accountability. Featured in this portion of the book are several accountability group models, including the author's "27:17 Model" (chap. 9 and Appendix A).

The kind of living and loving Christian community that this volume encourages is indeed achievable, but not without a price. At least three ingredients are necessary:
• acceptance of the wonderful love and grace of God
• a loving, supportive, small group of Christians
• a heart and mind open to change

If these three ingredients characterize you, or at least you want them to, read on! You may never be the same!

Bulletin Board

Consult with him that is wise and conscientious and seek to be instructed by a better than thyself, rather than to follow thine own inventions. (Thomas à Kempis)

We are grateful for the biblical teaching, underscored in the Reformation, that "there is . . . one mediator between God and men, the man Jesus Christ" (1 Tim. 2:5). We are also grateful for the biblical teaching, newly appreciated in our day, to "confess your sins to one another, and pray for one another . . . " (James 5:16, NASB). (Richard Foster)

God is calling into being a church that can openly confess its frail humanity and know the forgiving and empowering graces of Christ. (Richard Foster)

If thou intendest heartily to serve God, and avoid sin in any one instance, refuse not the hardest and most severe advice that is prescribed in order to it. (Jeremy Taylor)

If you choose to lay your anxiety before . . . some trusty and devout friend, you may be sure that you will find great solace. (Francis of Sales)

CHAPTER ONE

The Accountable Lifestyle

S everal years ago my wife and I were barreling down the interstate when I noticed for the first time what has become a common message on the back of trucks. The eighteen-wheeler owned by an Arkansas company bore the following dispatch:

> If you see this truck operating
> in an unsafe manner, call
> 1-800-555-3204

I am delighted that this company and an increasing number of others have added a new dimension of accountability to highway driving. That little message, it seemed to me, would serve as a ready deterrent to reckless driving by the "big rigs" if indeed their employers were serious about heeding the proffered comments. This particular organization recognized that commendation and censure are helpful in the pursuit of improved performance.

Not long after that I was again zipping down the highway when I found myself behind another freight mover that seemed to operate with a bit more reckless abandon. The truck bore a similar sign:

> Tell My Safety Department
> How I'm Doing!

There was a big difference, however, between this truck and the last one I had encountered. In this case the telephone number which motorists were to dial had been scraped off the back door of the vehicle. "Accountability!" the truck cried, but with no means to carry out the directive.

It caused me to reflect on accountability in our Christian lives and in the church. In recent years "accountability" has been on the lips and hearts of many evangelicals and has been the heart-cry of churches everywhere. Recent ethical lapses in Christian circles have convinced us all that we need to step up our level of accountability, as both institutions and individuals. But few people have provided practical, helpful means to implement accountability. Like the second truck, we have shouted yes to the need for purifying and strengthening relationships that would sharpen our witness. Too often, however, we have not taken specific measures toward such a commitment and thus, for all practical purposes we have whispered no with our lives.

Practical progress toward accountability is what this book is all about. As a first step, the wise course of action is to search out the biblical basis of the concept and work from there to a plan of responsible practice.

The Nature of God
A necessary first lesson in understanding God is understanding His essential nature. We need to know this because we have been made in the "image of God" (Gen. 1:27). If we want to become more like Him, we must understand what He is like.

God is Three. God is One. These seemingly paradoxical ideas are affirmed in Scripture and are part of the divine mystery. Scripture affirms that God, in essence, is a community (Three) and yet a unity (One). Made in His image, we are called to somehow reflect that reality.

"Hear, O Israel: The Lord our God, the Lord is One" (Deut. 6:4). This well-known verse proclaims the oneness of God. One scholar recently suggested that a closely related verse could be found in Psalm 133:1: "How good and pleasant it is when brothers live together in unity!" How are these passages related? The Hebrew words 'ehad (one) and yahad (unity) are closely identified in meaning, stressing, said the scholar, diversity within oneness.

As the Father, Son, and Holy Spirit are distinct Persons with diverse roles within the one Godhead, so we are called,

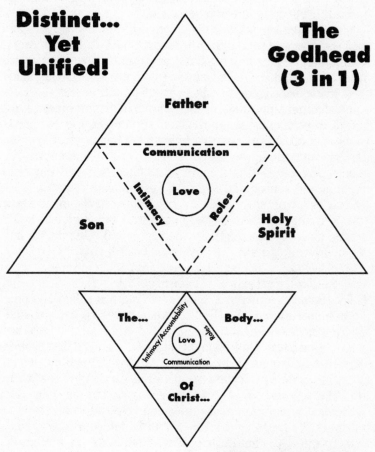

**Distinct...
Yet
Unified!**

**The
Godhead
(3 in 1)**

**The Church:
Reflecting the
Nature of
God**

as distinct individuals with diverse roles, to be bound together for a unified purpose—that of growing in Christlikeness and enlarging His kingdom. As a community of unity we are to hold one another accountable to, individually and corporately, reflecting the image of God.

Queen Victoria, as a child, evidently did not understand that she was in line for the throne of England. Her mentors, exasperated at her lethargic and unmotivated behavior, were at wits' end to discover a way to mold her into the young lady they knew she needed to be. One day, one of her teachers convinced her entourage of instructors that they must reveal her destiny as Queen of England. Upon hearing the news which had up to now been withheld from her, Victoria pursed her lips and then, with great resolve said, "Then I will be good!" She realized her destiny and that provided powerful impetus and a profound sense of responsibility.

Men and women of God are no different. We must know what the image of God is, recognize it as our high and noble calling, discover the relational means toward achieving it, and obediently implement a program of discipleship.

The Biblical Pattern of Accountability

Throughout Scripture it is clear that God has called His people to be accountable to Himself. Adam and Eve, for instance, hiding from God in the Garden, heard Him ask, "Where are you?" (Gen. 3:9) Those words and God's subsequent action showed that sin had consequences and that mankind would be accountable for a relationship to the Almighty Creator. In the following chapter of this Genesis story, the surviving son of the next generation hears the same voice after his crime of murder: "Where is your brother?" (4:9) These primary questions continue to confront us today. Where are we in relationship to God? Where are we in relationship to our brothers and sisters? As the biblical characters, we are accountable for answers to these divine inquiries.

From Genesis on we see God directing and commanding His people to "Do" and "Don't." And when He reveals His intentions, He means business. The Mosaic Law spelled out responsibilities to God and to fellow members of the faith community. When the people obeyed, blessing followed.

When they rebelled, there was punishment. The prophetic voices of Israel also beckoned the people to accountability as they thundered these same emphases—return to God; do justice, love mercy, walk humbly with God. If there were ever to be any hope of fulfilling God's design for abundant individual and corporate life, the people must be accountable to God.

The Book of Proverbs, a collection of short and pithy sayings, contains many statements dealing with accountability in the family as well as in other relationships. One of the key themes of this book is the wisdom of heeding counsel and admonitions from other members of the household—the household of our families and of our faith. Proverbs highlights the need for accountability in such verses as:

Whoever loves discipline loves knowledge, but he who hates correction is stupid (12:1).

The way of a fool seems right to him, but a wise man listens to advice (12:15).

A fool spurns his father's discipline, but whoever heeds correction shows prudence (15:5).

A mocker resents correction; he will not consult the wise (15:12).

A rebuke impresses a man of discernment more than a hundred lashes a fool (17:10).

Listen to advice and accept instruction, and in the end you will be wise (19:20).

Rebuke a discerning man, and he will gain knowledge (19:25).

As iron sharpens iron, so one man sharpens another (27:17).

He who conceals his sins does not prosper, but whoever

confesses and renounces them finds mercy (28:13).

A man who remains stiff-necked after many rebukes will suddenly be destroyed—without remedy (29:1).

Discipline, correction, advice, consultation, discernment, instruction, sharpening, confession, and rebuke are all expressions of an accountability desirable for people trying to walk with God. And the further into the biblical account we progress, the more evident it is that God's design is not accountability to Himself alone; He uses *people* as instruments in this plan. As with most of God's work in the world, He chooses to work through human agents to accomplish His will. The people of God are a vital interpersonal link in the development of responsible Christian living.

Paul's metaphor of the body of Christ is powerful at this point. He declares that we are not only called together, but that we desperately need each other to function.

Now the body is not made up of one part but of many. If the foot should say "Because I am not a hand, I do not belong to the body," it would not for that reason cease to be part of the body. . . . The eye cannot say to the hand, "I don't need you!" . . . there should be no division in the body, but its parts should have equal concern for each other. If one part suffers, every part suffers with it; if one part is honored, every part rejoices with it (1 Cor. 12:14-26).

The hands, for instance, are liable for the eyes. And vice versa. We were not created for a separate existence, responsible only for ourselves. Skin and bones, ligaments and tendons, we are jointed together to move in God's direction. To make any progress in this walk of faith we must march as a unit, in unanimity of mind and heart. A sing-along I learned as a youth at summer camp celebrates this coexistence: "We really do, need each other. It takes the brothers and the sisters, to make us whole!"

Perhaps our greatest impetus to accountability is found in the life of Jesus Himself. It is significant that when the Son of

God came in the flesh His primary role was as a teacher, an itinerant rabbi, building His ministry into the lives of His students with the expectation that they would repeat the disciple-making process. A linchpin of the rabbinic method, the method Jesus adopted, was accountability — the master holding his pupils accountable to learn certain lessons — in Jesus' case the lessons of the kingdom. But there was more. The rabbinic method also included the pupils holding one another accountable to follow after the instructor. A contemporary call to Christlikeness must apply both aspects of accountability: to the Teacher and to fellow followers.

Jesus' disciples apparently learned this lesson well, making accountability within the community of believers an integral part of the early church's worship. The house churches of the fledgling Christian movement practiced the confession of sins to each other. It is no mistake that we hear echoes of such activity in James' letter: "Confess your sins to each other and pray for each other so that you may be healed" (James 5:16).

Early church history so resonates with the principle of accountability that the apostles must certainly have modeled it in word and deed. In the *Didache* or *The Lord's Teaching by the Twelve Apostles to the Gentiles,* a church document dating from the first century, we read that confession was indeed a continuing tradition in the earliest centuries of Christianity.

In church, confess your transgressions, and do not go to prayer with an evil conscience.

On the Lord's own day come together, break bread and give thanks, but first confess your transgressions so that your offering may be pure.[1]

Interpersonal accountability was also the rule for those new in the faith. Origen, an early church father, noted that:

Individuals are taught as hearers, and only when they have given ample proof that they want to lead a good life are they introduced into the community. Some of the Christians are appointed to watch over the lives and appraise the conduct of those who want to join them.

They refuse to receive into the community those who have become guilty of evil deeds, while they receive the others with great joy, making them better from day to day.[2]

Accountability indeed! For the early church it was the rite of initiation and a continuing commitment in the pursuit of a progressive holiness of heart and life.

Submission to other members of the kingdom movement was the port of entry as well as an ongoing pattern for those who wanted to proceed in this unique Jesus faith. But that word "submit" seems richer in the Greek language than it does in our English context. More than a militaristic, "Yes, sir! No, sir!" mentality, it actually meant "good for persuasion," "compliant," "open to reason," and "willing to learn." This pattern of meaning describes believers who were humble and vulnerable to each other in their quest to know and imitate the Master. And the early church provided avenues for its members to thus progress, hand in hand, in the faith: Confess sin to each other. Be willing to accept loving encouragement and correction from others. Work out your salvation in the context of community, profiting from the example and instruction of fellow pilgrims. As Tertullian—another early church father—would say, "Men are made, not born Christians. The Christian soul is always made, never naturally born."[3] In the first centuries of the Christian church, this process of "making souls" included accountability—to God and man.

Accountability as a Means of Grace

John Wesley described the "means of grace" as outward signs, words, or actions, ordained of God and appointed to be the ordinary channels whereby He might convey to us His grace.[4] Simply, relational accountability is not an end in itself but a means by which to open ourselves to the grace which God provides. Unfortunately, these "means of *grace*," intended to draw us to God, can easily degenerate into mere *legalism*. Some churches try accountability groups and fail miserably simply because the issue becomes control: over the money, the schedules, the decisions and, ultimately, the lives of others. Thus the paradox: what was intended to bring liberty instead engenders bondage. Such groups give accountability a bad name.

But when accountability is truly seen—as a way that God can shed grace, mercy, and power in our lives—it becomes liberating, joyous, and broadening. Through interaction with Scripture and with fellow believers we learn to be more Christlike; to act with the best interests of the other person in mind; to meet problems together; to suggest solutions rather than demand compliance.

The Liberation of Accountability

I invited my friend Jody to come and share in a class entitled "Discipleship in the Home." I wanted my students to hear how scarred by sin—and not always our own—an individual can be, and how free we can become in Christ. I excerpt a few of Jody's opening remarks:

> I'm afraid I'm going to blow you out of your socks. Some of the things that go on in homes today are astounding. . . . My sobriety date is May 23, 1981. I'm an adult child of two alcoholics. I'm a survivor of child abuse and child sexual abuse. I drank twenty-one years and was addicted to prescription drugs for seven. I've seriously attempted suicide two times. Once with drugs, once with gunshot. I've been in numerous psychiatric hospitals and have been diagnosed as paranoid schizophrenic, manic depressive, and have had eighteen shock treatments. I also have an eating disorder—anorexia and bulimia. People like me tend to grow up to be alcoholics and drug addicts, marry them, or both. I get to mark all of the above.

I had already informed my class that Jody was a valued friend of my family and the frequent baby-sitter of my infant son. It made them all the more eager to discover how in the world she had recovered from such a debilitating start in life. Her reply was simple and can be expressed in two emphases that are inseparable—accountability and Jesus Christ. Having other people to encourage her and hold her to the commitment to salvation and sobriety was a key factor in Jody's recovery. As she says today, "I believe that God now has a purpose for my life, and that He's going to make something really beautiful out of something that started really ugly."

Knowing what Jody *was* like and what she is now, I would say that accountability to an intimate small group and Jesus Christ were her only hope. And mark it well—her life has been redeemed. She now serves in a ministry of recovery to hurting people who have suffered similar life circumstances. She is a leader in our church. And she is a constant help and blessing to her friends and her community. Hers is a story of healing, of brokenness made whole.

Jody had problems that many of us have and that many of us do not. But we have *all* been marred by sin and because of this are less than God wants us to be. We can never begin to reach our full potential for His kingdom without accountability to God and man.

One important caution. In the New Testament church, as Eduard Schweizer points out, accountability was more than mere haggling over sin in general and habitual faults in particular. Again and again in the small congregations the call to "live anew, and better" was the constant encouragement.

It is always looking forwards, always at the open door to the new week in which once again it may live—and much better than in the week just gone—on what has been given to it. It does not look back full of remorse. It has renounced sin by building its life on God's gracious action, and so it is no longer possible for it, even if there were time, to revolve pharisaically round its good deeds, or penitently round bad ones.[5]

Accountability in the church was meant to release people from the shortcomings of their pasts and help them build God-centered futures. That was, and is, the beauty of the process. Accountability sets us free to fly! Once a particular sin is confessed and repented of, it can be released to God and the believer can go forward victorious over those defeats of sin and failure.

I am often reminded of the Hebrew word for salvation—

yasha — with cognates meaning "to make wide," "roomy," "to be well off," "to be free," "prosperous." The word *Yeshua* — Hebrew for Jesus — comes from the same word group. That challenges me. What our Lord really wants for us is a widening of our lives; a freedom that launches us toward wellness and increase. But we must remember, as Jesus suggested, that "narrow is the way" to such broadening. Accountability is one of the narrow "ways." And God has ordained the necessary ingredients to make His dream for us reality: the grace of God through Jesus Christ, the intimacy of a small group, confession, change, and healing. As we appropriate His plan and provision for us, God is able to make us into all we were meant to be, doing all we were meant to do!

When I was at Kansas University, some older guys working for a campus ministry challenged me to join them in Bible study, prayer, and learning the lessons of discipleship that were crucial to maintaining a Christian witness on campus. I joined them for a while, but before long I floated away, uninterested in such a regimen. I look back over the last three decades and consider that discipleship group as one of the major missed opportunities of my life. What they asked of me was simple: come to weekly meetings; work, play, and pray with them; hold each other accountable for how well we stood for Christ in our example and witness on a day-to-day basis. I vowed that the next time such an opportunity came along, I wouldn't miss it.

The opportunity did come, in seminary. I threw myself into relationships with my accountability groups, and I grew tremendously as a Christian. We covenanted together to pray and study Scripture for a certain amount of time each day. We memorized Bible verses. We prayed, and argued, and shared insights. We vowed to ask each other the tough questions when needed. My life has never been the same. The positive impact of this group and the pattern it set for my life inspires me to do everything I can to encourage others to participate in small group accountability.

Why Not Accountability?

If we recognize accountable relationships as being both biblically based and vital to the integrity of our Christian faith, why have we been reticent to invite others into our lives to love, encourage, correct, and exhort? Some common excuses:

"But I am accountable! To God!"

After my talks and sermons on accountability no response is more common than this. It generally indicates a bit of defensiveness and a reluctance to help build a genuine community. I said the same thing when I wanted to pursue God but certainly didn't want anybody else nitpicking about things that I may or may not have considered crucial to a life of holiness.

It's true that we are accountable to God for our relationship with Him. Prayer, the reading and memorization of Scripture, and heeding the gentle (and not so gentle!) nudges of the Holy Spirit are all important means of knowing and obeying Him which no one else can do for us. But too often we attempt to meet our need for accountability at the divine level only, discounting God's design that we be held accountable by Him *and* His body, the church. Both are vital. Both are necessary. I am reminded of the familiar story of a little girl calling from her bedroom on a stormy night. "Mommy, I'm scared. Please come here!" From the living room, the mother comforted her daughter, replying, "God is with you." After several moments the child replied, "I know that. But, Mommy, I need somebody with some skin on!"

God is with us. But the little girl was on target. We need those somebodies with "skin on," and God provides them in His body, the community of believers.

"I did it my *way!"*

Thomas Jefferson, from the birth of the United States of America, proposed that one of the goals and rights of our life together is the pursuit of happiness. In our society, suggests Tom Sine, that translates as the *individualistic pursuit of happiness,* and that "an authentic study of the Gospels shows us that the individualistic pursuit of happiness should not be the life goal of a Christian. In fact, it would be difficult to find a goal for human life that is more antithetical to everything Jesus represented."[6]

Sine's comments on this issue caused me to consider our

goals in the Christian life. We tend to make the pursuit of
holiness, the noblest of objectives, an individualistic endeavor.
We urge people to "invite Jesus Christ into your hearts as
personal Savior." Perhaps we have used this lingo so much
that we have forgotten an important corollary: an invitation to
an intimate, personal relationship with Jesus is also a call to
intimacy with His body. That involves community. That involves us — together.

One church in our city makes an altar call nearly every
Sunday for those who want to receive Christ and be placed on
the membership rolls. As the respondents are signing their
cards — name, address, telephone number — an associate pastor whispers in their ear: "You know, of course, that when
you join this church you are committing yourself to full involvement in the Sunday School and tithing programs as
well?" As one of those associates related to me, "When we
say that, they either blink, laugh faintly, and try to save face,
or they look you straight in the eye and say, 'Let's go!' " In
our own evangelism perhaps we, along with the Holy Spirit
and Scripture, should whisper in the newcomer's ear: "You
need the empowering, correcting, loving, intimate relationships of other believers in your life. Sign on with Him, and
you're signing on with the community of believers as well!"

A call to the Christian faith ought also to mean that we
recognize Jesus as the Head of a body, and ourselves as
members. That implies many things, not the least of which is
accountable relationships.

"I'm afraid to tell you who I am."

This is a common rationale for reluctance — and sometimes
for good reason. "What will happen if I let them know where
I stand, what my shortcomings and failures are, where I need
help? Will they laugh? Be bored? Lose respect for me? Be
angry? Will they break confidence and tell someone else?
What if I have to change — quit doing something — begin doing
something . . . that I don't want to?"

Most of these are natural fears and not entirely misplaced.
Let's be frank — accountability relationships are dangerous. If
not handled responsibly, relationships of any kind — including
intense spiritual ones — can result in damaged emotions, hurt

feelings, and squelched spirituality.

But a lack of accountability is even more dangerous. Without it we will not make optimal progress toward our God-given potentials. And worse, blinded to our own pitfalls we may lose ground spiritually if we neglect the life-to-life sharpening of our characters and actions which others can provide.

A church was constructed in Hillsboro, Illinois in 1903; by 1987 that ecclesiastical edifice had taken on the name "Church Street Pub"—a bar and restaurant. The stained-glass windows remain, but the Sunday School room now houses a bar. Plans are in the works to make the pulpit a stage; the pews are to be cleared out to make way for a dance floor. Dale Lingle, owner of the pub, notes a conspicuous absence, however. Two pictures of Jesus, once featured in the sanctuary windows, have been taken down and donated to a local church. Lingle observes, "Having Him in here would make me feel real uncomfortable!"

Interesting comment. Having Jesus, and those whom He provides to keep us sharp and pure, is occasionally uncomfortable. There may well be times when we wish that Jesus, or His saints, weren't there probing and loving, challenging and pleading. But the bottom line is that we have nothing to fear from the presence of Christ or His body. They are intended to benefit us.

I have always loved this exchange about Jesus in Lloyd C. Douglas' classic *The Robe*. The character Marcellus asks Justus after Christ's ascension, "Where do you think He went?"

"I don't know, my friend. I only know that He is alive—and I am always expecting to see Him. Sometimes I feel aware of Him, as if He were close by." Justus smiled faintly, his eyes wet with tears. "It keeps you honest," he went on. "You have no temptation to cheat anyone, or to lie to anyone, or hurt anyone—when, for all you know, Jesus is standing beside you."

"I'm afraid I should feel very uncomfortable," remarked Marcellus, "being perpetually watched by some invisible presence."

"Not if that presence helped you defend yourself against yourself, Marcellus. It is a great satisfaction to have someone standing by—to keep you at your best."[7]

Accountable relationships—someone standing by to keep us at our best! From that perspective accountability becomes refreshing and a means toward the kind of life we truly desire.

"What?/So what?"

A pollster was assigned to approach a hundred people on the streets of his city and ask the question, "Would you agree— yes or no—that the major problems of the general populace of this nation are ignorance and apathy?" The terse reply of one fellow, accompanied by a cold shoulder, perfectly matched the question. He answered, "I don't know and I don't care!"

A lack of knowledge and concern about spiritual growth leads to mediocrity. More and more people level that accusation at contemporary Western Christianity. And mediocre is a telling and interesting word. It comes from the Latin *medius* for "middle" and *ocris* for "peak." The picture that arises is of a mountain climber who has ascended halfway to the mountaintop. Perhaps he has pitched his tent and occasionally emerges to gauge the distance to the top and to remind himself how far he has come. Satisfied at his progress and quite content to stay where he is, the erstwhile climber slips back into the tent to remain just halfway up the mountain.

We run the risk of settling for less than the peak, the intended objective, in our Christian lives without colleagues in the faith straining and pulling, pushing and prodding to help us reach the goal.

A.W. Tozer addressed stalled, complacent Christians when he said:

I want deliberately to encourage [a] mighty longing after God. The lack of it has brought us to our present low estate. The stiff and wooden quality about our religious lives is a result of our lack of holy desire. . . . Complacency is a deadly foe of all spiritual growth. Acute desire must be present or there will be no manifestation of Christ to His people. He waits to be wanted.

Too bad that with many of us He waits so long, so very long, in vain.[8]

"I don't know and I don't care" is not the heart cry of those who truly desire Christian excellence. Teamwork toward the top—toward the waiting Christ—is. That is what accountability is all about.

"I don't need it!"

Many of us probably pick up a volume like this one and think to ourselves, "I know someone who needs to read that book." The implication is that we know other people who are messing up their lives and could sure use someone to straighten them out. We never once think, "I need accountability to help make *me* more Christlike." But we all need it. All of us.

One of my friends made an intriguing comment about the title of James Dobson's best-selling book, *Dare to Discipline*. Lamenting the declining moral values of the Christian church he noted, "What we really need today is someone to write a book called *Dare to Be Disciplined*. We need to get a fresh vision of what it means to ask others into our lives to help us be the disciplined disciples God intends!" When talking about what "we need," he meant *all of us*. And he is right.

At the NCAA Track and Field Championships my final year in college, I gathered with a number of athletes and coaches to watch the shot put competition. The discus, my event, was over and I had finished toward the top of the pack, but not high enough for my liking. I was half-watching, half-lamenting that my career was now over, when an athlete from another university looked over at me. He told me what one of the most prominent coaches in the nation, sitting right in front of us, had said about me during the discus contest: "Did you know that Tom Tellez said that if you could just get rid of that little hop in the middle of your spin, you could sure throw a lot farther."

"What!" I said. Tellez, *the* Tellez, thought I could have thrown a lot farther if I had better form. To be frank, I didn't know whether to be elated or angry. Why hadn't my coach, the famous and much respected Bob Timmons, told me?

More than a little disgusted, I asked Coach Timmons about it later. He reminded me, much to my chagrin, that over and over he had tried to change my wretched form, including that little hop, but that I had always replied, "But, Coach, that's just part of my *style!*" It hit me like a ton of bricks. Now I remembered. Despite my coach's efforts, I had thumbed my nose at correction. As a result, I still don't know how far I *could have thrown* had I listened and accepted the sharpening advice of Coach Timmons.

The moral of that story transfers easily to the spiritual aspect of our lives. In the things that really matter, have we made the decision to heed the advice, the words, the correction, the coaching that we really need to hear? Can any of us fulfill our spiritual potential without it? As Tozer reminds us, we won't be judged for what we did or didn't do, but for what we could have done. We can, and should, approach our potential with "coaches" who correct us and cheer us on to new heights of Christian living.

Who needs accountability most? *Everybody* needs it most, for none has progressed as far in the Christian faith as he could have, or should have. No one should be found absent from God's training ground of accountability.

"Later. . . . "

If Tozer is right about complacency being a deadly foe of spiritual growth, then its close cousin is procrastination. Few would argue against the necessity of accountability for an effective, commissioned church. The problem lies with setting a starting point in our own lives. Today, not tomorrow, is the day to begin.

But a move from talk to action is a bold, and often avoided, step. To be accountable to someone, we must swerve from our paths, from our own agendas, from the normal way of doing things. We must change, and change is hard. To paraphrase Augustine, we say, "Lord, give me accountability, but not yet!"

Keith Drury has written a helpful pamphlet on "How to Establish Accountability" in which he speaks to this issue of procrastination as it exists in the everyday life of the Christian. He argues that Christians are used to making commitments, and then just as easily breaking them. An endless cycle of commitment, failure, repentance, and then a repeat commitment is defeating. Eventually, people and whole churches simply quit making those commitments. Drury prophetically exhorts such individuals and congregations with these words:

> Then why haven't you started? I suspect procrastination is the most common excuse. . . .
>
> What is the remedy for procrastination? Accountability. But if you are a procrastinator, you are probably procrastinating on taking the cure. . . . Procrastinators especially need accountability. It's the antidote for this disorder of your will. . . .
>
> Action breaks the bindings of procrastination. So start now. Do something. As soon as you lay down this article. Go ahead . . . break the shackles of procrastination by taking action. The reason you have become such a procrastinator is your habit of reading or listening to great ideas you'd like to do, but never taking action on them. It's time to change all that. Today.[9]

The procrastinator is halfway up the mountain. Now is the time to begin setting your eyes toward reaching the peak. Today.

"But I've never seen it work."

It's true! Role models in accountability are hard to come by, perhaps because there has tended to be a lack of this kind of relationship in American Christendom. That we must change. But the other side of the issue is simply that those who have found a workable system of accountability often practice it effectively but quietly. In chapter 9 some models of effective accountability will be presented for you to consider.

A Need We Must Address

In the spring of 1983 the National Commission on Excellence in Education delivered a stinging report on the state of education in the United States. A few excerpts became etched in the national psyche.

Our nation is at risk. . . . As it stands, we have allowed this to happen to ourselves. . . . We have, in effect, been committing an act of unthinking, unilateral educational disarmament.

The Commission's assessment is today echoed by Christian leaders and laypeople. But now it's different, for the criticism is being leveled at the church. "At risk!" many saints lament. The church has "disarmed!" say others. There are many who detect a crisis of integrity and therefore of effectiveness in the church. In the words of Archibald D. Hart of Fuller Theological Seminary the problem is not so much a product of "blatant dishonesty as a tendency toward autonomy and independence."

There is a tendency in all of us to want to avoid being subjected to control by others. . . . Accountability to another, even when you are the top leader of an organization or church, is the only way to safeguard against poor judgment, unconscious motivations, and self-deception. And that accountability must be regular, personal, face-to-face, honest, and transparent.[10]

Avoiding the drift away from Christian integrity, a constant undertow that would put us at risk, requires accountability that is, as Cox says . . .
- regular
- personal
- face-to-face
- honest
- transparent

And it must address issues vital to our lives under God, such as those included in the following chapters: inner life, mission, money, sex, health, family, and daily Christian living. In hopes of helping both lay and clergy get a handle on how to initiate an accountable lifestyle, practical techniques and patterns for accountability are discussed.

The challenge of the next several chapters of this handbook is to explore some areas of our lives that need change and investigate ways we might make ourselves personally accountable. Chapter 9 and the appendixes can help you establish a life-changing accountability group.

A challenge: don't skip a chapter. *USA Today* ran an ad for a tanning salon franchise years ago that stated simply: "OWN A SLICE OF THE SUN." I have often compared that to some people's Christianity. We want to accept a slice of the Son, or a slice of the way He wants us to live. That is a dangerous tactic and will lead us to be less than God wants us to be. Plato once said that it is easy to forgive a child afraid of the dark, but the real tragedy of life is when adults are afraid of the light. The intention of this book is simply to shed some light on areas that, if aligned with biblical priorities, will help us maximize our lives for Jesus Christ.

Bulletin Board

If you can beat the devil in the matter of daily prayer, you can beat him anywhere. But if he can beat you there, he possibly can beat you anywhere. (Paul Rader)

The man who has no inner life "is the slave of his surroundings." (Henri Frederic Amiel)

The meaning of earthly existence is not, as we have grown used to thinking, in prosperity, but in the development of the soul. (Aleksandr Solzhenitsyn)

. . . if we do not give our time and our earnest longing to find Christ in the silence of our inner lives, then we shall lose our true life altogether. We may gain other things, but we shall lose the best thing of all. (Charles F. Andrews)

Devotion is neither private nor public prayer, but a life given to God. He is the devout man, therefore, who considers and serves God in everything and who makes all of his life an act of devotion by doing everything in the name of God and under such rules as are conformable to His glory. (William Law)

CHAPTER TWO

Devotional Life

Ionce showed up at an evening church service with two tree branches. One of them had been cut recently and still showed evidence of thick green foliage; the other, after lying on the ground beneath the tree for untold months, looked very dry and dead. I held the limbs in front of the congregation and asked, "What is the difference between the two?" Answer: one was dead, shriveled up, ugly, good for burning; the other was leafy, alive, and you wouldn't think of using it in the fireplace. The audience recognized the correspondence between the branches before them and the words of Jesus:

> Abide in Me, and I in you. As the branch cannot bear fruit of itself, unless it abides in the vine, neither can you, unless you abide in Me. I am the vine, you are the branches. He who abides in Me, and I in him, bears much fruit; for without Me you can do nothing. If anyone does not abide in Me, he is cast out as a branch and is withered; and they gather them and throw them into the fire, and they are burned (John 15:4-6, NKJV).

The sermon for the evening: spirituality is all about connectedness—staying attached to and drawing life from God.

That is a continuing challenge for modern-day disciples. Staying connected and fortifying our devotional lives is unfamiliar territory to many of us, for frequently we have not been taught nor have we developed the conviction that this endeavor is a primal concern of our faith. Several centuries ago the reformer Luther said of his country that "all churches and monastic houses are full of praying and singing, but how does it happen that so little improvement and benefit result from it, and things daily grow worse?"[1] While Luther was concerned about full pews, contemporary pastor Charlie Shedd has a different worry. "Pews built for people, but nobody in them. Yet the real tragedy is not those empty pews. It's empty people."[2]

Full pews or empty, the real concern should be lives wholly devoted to God. Let's investigate some beginning steps toward that objective.

Step One

Once you have made a commitment to Jesus Christ as Lord and Savior, the first step in developing a framework for spiritual growth is habitual communion with God. Such communion—or lack of it—may well be our greatest weakness in evangelical America. Research supports the conclusion that few people have the kind of daily communion with God that has traditionally been regarded necessary for the deeper life. Given the average time spent by Christians in prayer and Bible study, the song entitled "Sweet Hour of Prayer" might better be rendered "Sweet Moment of Panicked Petition" or "Sweet Dinnertime Thanks." We have lost the art of extended periods of communication with the Almighty and Holy God. We must reclaim the disciplines that lead us to Him.

The two foundational spiritual exercises for the cultivation of the inner life are prayer and Bible study. A graph of my spiritual history would undoubtedly show that the peaks always occurred when the disciplines of daily prayer and Bible study/meditation were both being practiced regularly. The valleys would indicate their inconsistency or absence. To develop our souls we must pray. To develop our souls we must read and be formed by Scripture. Let's explore each of these essentials of spiritual growth.

Prayer

E. Stanley Jones notes that:

> Where there is no effective prayer life, the heart of religion has ceased to beat and religion becomes a dead body of forms and customs and dogmas. And yet how

few Christians have an effective prayer life! If I were to put my finger on the greatest lack in American Christianity, I would unhesitatingly point to the need for an effective prayer life among laity and ministers.[3]

Jones was talking about a set-apart time—a significant item on the daily schedule where one's focus turns wholeheartedly to communion with the Creator. He notes in his autobiography, *A Song of Ascents,* that one of the best things he ever did in college was establish a daily, two-hour prayer habit. It served him well throughout a long, fruitful missionary career. And, said the famous Bishop J.C. Ryle, saints through the ages have shared this "secret."

I have read the lives of many eminent Christians who have been on earth since the Bible days. Some of them, I see, were rich, and some poor. Some were learned, some unlearned. Some of them were Episcopalians, and some Christians of other denominations. Some were Calvinists, and some were Arminians. Some have loved to use a liturgy, and some chose to use none. But one thing, I see, they all had in common. They all have been men of prayer.[4]

Years ago a science periodical featured an article on prescription drugs. The author described a central supposition often overlooked in our lay understanding of medicine: no drug has *just* a central effect. There are always side effects. And frequently, the drug that we take for a particular ailment will noticeably impact our whole person. I think this pharmaceutical characteristic applies to prayer as well. The primary purpose of prayer is communication with God. But that communication is more than a verbal exchange. Coming into contact with the Almighty changes us; His presence impacts our attitudes, our activities, our decisions, and priorities.

Anthropologists, in the study of religious cultures, differentiate between magic and religion. They examine both primitive and sophisticated cultures and see magical tendencies—the attempt of people to manipulate the gods or god to accomplish their desires. Religion, on the other hand, occurs when people seek to discover and do the divine will. That distinction helps me when I think in terms of prayer. Am I praying, "Lord, get on my side of the issue, do this or that, I just know that it's the right thing"? Or am I praying, "Lord, I love You. What is Your will? How can I be a part of Your plans? How can I change to be used by You?" Scripture is full of people praying bold prayers, asking God for mighty things. But could the dramatic results reflect the fact that these men and women were first attuned to what God desired, and prayed accordingly? The greatest effect of prayer is to align us with God (to love, praise, and know Him) and His purposes (to think, plan, do with Him).

Patterns of prayer. In seeking to develop our prayer lives we need to remember that Jesus prayed often, regularly, even ritualistically, if we assume that Jesus held to the rich Jewish patterns of prayer and praise. He beckons us to follow. While the forms we use may differ, we will find it impossible to be Christlike in any significant and enduring way without pursuing this avenue of spiritual growth.

Perhaps one of the best places to begin a study of prayer is the familiar Lord's Prayer that Jesus taught the disciples. Here E. Stanley Jones discovered a dynamic that is interesting in light of the "alignment" aspect of prayer already noted.[5] Working with the pronouns of the prayer, he noticed that there seemed to be two distinct and important movements.

Our Father in heaven, hallowed be *Your name, Your kingdom* come, *Your will* be done on earth as it is in heaven. *Give us* today our daily bread. *Forgive us* our debts, as we also have forgiven our debtors. And *lead us* not into temptation, but *deliver us* from the evil one.

The two sides of the prayer, as Jones sees it, are the realignment side and the result side.

REALIGNMENT	RESULT
Our Father	Give us
Your name	Forgive us
Your kingdom	Lead us
Your will	Deliver us

In the first section, we realign our lives to "Our Father": to His name, His kingdom, His will. In the second, we get the result: He gives to us, forgives us, leads us, delivers us. These are the alternate beats of the heart of prayer... realignment-result, realignment-result. We get as much result as we have realignment. The more we realign, the greater the results. This is not a magical formula but a pattern built into the universe: "The prayer of a righteous man [i.e., *rightly aligned*] is powerful and effective" (James 5:16).

The Lord's Prayer can be used to structure a significant portion of devotional time. Meditate and pray through each of the eight segments and allow God to speak to you. Take the words "Our Father" and drink deeply. Praise the Father for who Scripture reveals Him to be; thank Him for His liberating acts in history and in your life; think of particular qualities that He impresses on your heart to emulate. Move on to the remainder of the "realignment" parts of the prayer: ask how you can align yourself with His holy name, His kingdom, His will. On the "result" side, ask that He give you what you need for your daily kingdom endeavor, that He forgive you of recognized sins, that He lead you — not just *from* sin but *to* righteousness, and deliver you from the evil that might attack you that day.

There are other helpful patterns of prayer. The acronym "ACTS" is one of the most familiar:

Adoration of the Father, Son, and Holy Spirit,
Confession of sin,
Thanksgiving for God's many blessings, and
Supplication, or asking requests of God.

In his book *The Hour That Changes the World,* Dick Eastman describes a twelve-part pattern for spending an hour in prayer. He recommends devoting five minutes daily to each of these twelve steps: (1) praise, (2) waiting, (3) confession, (4) Scripture praying, (5) watching, (6) intercession, (7) petition, (8) thanksgiving, (9) singing, (10) meditation, (11) listening, (12) praise.[6]

There is no one right way to pray. But giving structure to the time of prayer helps many of us not only learn the discipline of private devotion, but continue in it as well. Different personalities will prefer different approaches to communion with God. Some will feel more comfortable taking an early morning prayer walk in the park, others will prefer a prayer closet. Some like to write out their prayers in journals; others need vocal conversation. Imagery works for many, liturgy helps others. The point is, we need to find a way of approaching God and aligning our lives with Him that is daily, consistent, and personally enriching.

To establish an ongoing "quiet time" of praise, confession, thanksgiving, and intercession, is a key component for the person committed to developing godly character and service.

Bible study

Chuck Yeager, the famed pilot, was flying an F-86 Sabre over a lake in the Sierras when he decided to buzz a friend's house near the edge of the lake. During a slow roll, he suddenly felt an aileron lock. Says Yeager, "It was a hairy moment, flying about 150 feet off the ground and upside down." A lesser pilot might have panicked with fatal results, but Yeager let off on the Gs, pushed up the nose and sure enough, the aileron unlocked. Climbing to 15,000 feet, where it was safer, Yeager tried the maneuver again. Every time he rolled the problem reoccurred. Yeager knew that three or four pilots had died under similar circumstances, but to date investigators were puzzled as to the source of the Sabre's fatal flaw.

Yeager went to his superior with a report and the inspectors went to work. They found that a bolt on the aileron cylinder had been installed upside down. Eventually, the culprit was found in a North American plant. He was an older man on the assembly line who ignored instructions about how to insert that bolt, because he knew that bolts were supposed to be placed head up, not head down. In a sad commentary, Yeager says that nobody ever told the man how many pilots he killed.[7]

The Bible contains our instructions. We should know what those instructions say and apply their directives immediately to our lives. As we do so, there are two basic approaches to the study of Scripture. One is *informational*, concerned primarily with content. The other is *formational*, a more meditative approach which concentrates on a small section of the Bible, perhaps even a single word or verse. Most of us, by virtue of our personalities and learning styles, have a natural propensity toward one of these approaches. But both aspects of Scripture study are vital—either one, without the other, will result in a deficiency in our devotional diet and thus will stunt our spiritual growth.

Informational. Mastery of biblical content is essential to the Christian life. Where else will we find out what God wants us to be and do? Our ability to grow in obedience and Christlikeness will be severely limited if we remain ignorant of the instruction and encouragement God has provided in the Bible. Our challenge is to diligently examine Scripture. Some suggestions:

- Follow one of several plans for reading through the Bible. As you read several chapters at a time, try to get a feel for the style of the author. Perhaps use several translations and a good study Bible.
- Trace major themes as they flow from Genesis through Revelation: the holiness of God, the problem of sin, God's plan of redemption, etc.
- Study individual books: When were they written? Why? By whom? Why has God placed these words here? What is the main idea(s)? How do the parts (verses, chapters, sections) fit together to make the whole?

Engaging in these or similar plans can lay a vital foundation for understanding our calling in Christ. But beware—knowing the content does not equal spiritual growth. It is possible to rattle off summaries of all sixty-six books, to have all kinds of doctrinal knowledge and background information on biblical times, and remain untouched and unchanged in the depths of our souls. For this reason we need to emphasize the formational process as well.

Formational. This approach to Scripture focuses on savoring smaller portions—one incident or parable, perhaps a single verse, or even a word. We intentionally limit our scope in order to move beyond glib explanations. Take time to mull over the words of the passage—sometimes they have become so familiar that we are startled to discover "new" truths that have been there all along. What is God saying through this passage? How does it impact your life?

A devotional attitude toward Scripture is a vital link in spiritual growth—this is God's Living Word with something to say to our present situation. But beware: this approach could become very subjective if not grounded in the facts, complemented by the informational side of Bible study. It is possible to take a few verses and come up with an entirely skewed conclusion about God, His intentions, or ourselves if we neglect the context in which those verses appear.

We need an integrated approach to Bible study, one that combines a "clearheaded" grasp of the whole message of Scripture with a "warmhearted" devotion that applies truth to our lives to bring forth change. No single plan can claim a corner on the market, but Appendix E has two approaches that have been helpful to many students of the Word.

In Scripture it is noted that Ezra devoted himself to *study,* and *observance,* and to *teaching* the decrees and laws he had learned (Ezra 7:10). Study—Do it—Hand it along: a good model to follow for those eager to "follow the instructions."

Beyond the Devotional Time

Establishing a daily time with God that includes Bible study and prayer is vital, but the development of our inner life cannot be confined to private moments alone with Him. All our moments—the people, events, and tasks we encounter— impact our spiritual health. In our actions and reactions we are moving either toward or away from Christlikeness. Once we come to grips with the fact that *everything* we do impacts our devotional lives, we approach life with a bit more holy awareness.

What changes us? Everything . . .

- That fight you had last night with your wife affected you spiritually.
- The television program that had you laughing this morning made a devotional impact.
- Reading the newspaper moments ago will ensure that you are never the same.
- The discussion you had on the phone right before you went to bed last night nudged you toward—or away from—God's kingdom.

- The Scripture and prayer you shared with your family —
  and the way you shared it — guarantees change.

Whether monumental or miniscule, life change from our everyday comings and goings is inevitable. While we should not become paranoid about the possible aftershock of our every little move, it is important to remember that we are to be about God's business in everything we do. C.S. Lewis was right. "We have no non-religious activities; only religious and irreligious."[8] We need to seize all moments as formational to our inner lives.

The ultimate goal is to incorporate an attitude of devotion into all of life. Concentrated times of prayer and Bible study ought to lead us to a moment-by-moment awareness of the Divine. One member of our congregation recently approached me about a small volume that she had checked out from our church library. "What do you know about the short work called *The Practice of the Presence of God?*" she asked. "I have really found it to be a fascinating and helpful book!" I explained that the book was, as she had undoubtedly already discovered, edited by a gentleman named M. Beaufort and contained conversations and letters of a lay brother in a Carmelite monastery. "Brother Lawrence," as he was known, demonstrated that daily living wedded with prayer is a real possibility. "The time of business does not with me differ from the time of prayer," says this brother, "and in the noise and clatter of my kitchen, while several persons are at the same time calling for different things, I possess God in as great tranquility as if I were upon my knees at the blessed sacrament."[9]

This small book has inspired countless people in the centuries since its publication because it speaks to the yearning we all feel to carry something of God with us into our every activity. A time of prayer, whether it be an hour, a half hour, or five minutes, is beneficial to our inner lives. But for Brother Lawrence, and for many of us, that is not enough. Beaufort notes that Brother Lawrence said of his own prayer life, "With him the set times of prayer were not different from other times; that he retired to pray, according to the directions of his superior, but that he did not want such retirement, nor ask for it, because his greatest business did not distract him from God."[10] Conversations, daily duties, washing pots and pans ... all should be done while "habitually practicing His presence" and "continually conversing with Him." Brother Lawrence thought "that it was a great delusion to think that the times of prayer ought to differ from other times; that we are as strictly obliged to adhere to God by action in the time of action as by prayer in the season of prayer."

That sets a high standard, to be sure. But I think it is attainable for all those who will ask God to help them and then set themselves to the joyous task of "practicing God's presence." To pray and meditate upon God's Word daily — in special hours and in our normal comings and goings — and to act on it, is a holy practice worth our noblest efforts.

Other Spiritual Disciplines
Other devotional practices can enhance our growth as well. Once the foundation of prayer and Bible study is in place and the disciple is working on God's abiding presence moment by moment, other avenues of grace to be explored include meditation, fasting, Scripture memory, and journaling, to name a few. Some of these devotional practices will prove to be more helpful than others, depending on the individual; the important thing is to get a spiritual growth mix that incorporates some of these disciplines and begins to launch you "out into the depths."

Certainly any newly acquired practice is far more easily implemented with the support and example of others. The premise of this book is that a small group whose members love and support each other is invaluable. The spiritual discipline of reading modern and classic works of devotional literature can also motivate and encourage us with inspired words and exemplary models. Below are a few suggestions to get you started:

Classics
A Serious Call to a Devout and Holy Life by William Law
The Practice of the Presence of God by Brother Lawrence
The Imitation of Christ by Thomas à Kempis
A Testament of Devotion by Thomas Kelly

Modern "helps"
The Hour That Changes the World by Dick Eastman
2959 Plan by Peter Lord
How to Pray by E. Stanley Jones
Shaped by the Word by Robert Mulholland
Power through Prayer by E.M. Bounds
Celebration of Discipline by Richard Foster
The Meaning of Prayer by Harry Emerson Fosdick

Devotionals
Look for those by Oswald Chambers, E. Stanley Jones, C.S. Lewis.

Biographies
John (Praying) Hyde, Rees Howells, John and Susannah Wesley, George Müller, William Carey, Amy Carmichael, Mother Teresa, Jim Elliot, Toyohiko Kagawa, Francis of Assisi, Augustine, heroes of faith in your denomination.

As you search the libraries at your disposal you will notice that some of these books are crusty and perhaps rather ancient-looking. But don't be dismayed just because the book cover doesn't reflect the slick technology of the last few decades. Albert Einstein, in *Ideas and Opinions,* noted:

> Somebody who reads only newspapers and at best books of contemporary authors looks to me like an extremely near-sighted person who scorns eyeglasses. He is completely dependent on the prejudices and fashions of his times, since he never gets to see or hear anything else.[11]

There is great value in tasting the old wine.

Who Is Doing the Forming?
Guy Lefrancois tells of a ploy by undergraduate psychology students. After lectures on B.F. Skinner regarding operant conditioning and behavioral shaping, Lefrancois and several other sly students attempted to corroborate the professor's words by an informal, semester-long experiment. Essentially, the lessons of the professor boiled down to this: rewarded or

reinforced behavior means the greater probability of continued behavior. So, a half dozen students decided to become "head nodders." As a graduate-level professor, I can tell you that a head nodder is a super reinforcer to a teacher. It echoes that yes, someone is listening and yes, they like what is being said.

The head nodders, however, nodded to affirm not the content but the professor's pacing. When he quit moving, they quit nodding. After only four lectures or so, says Lefrancois, the professor paced incessantly, to the delight of the six students. That accomplished, they decided to extinguish that behavior and reinforce lecturing from one corner of the room. This too was managed easily. The next step was to condition lecturing from another corner. They successfully achieved the desired behavior modification, and the professor never knew that his classroom manner was being conditioned by the smiles and nods of just a handful of students.[12]

I have to stop and ask: Who and what is forming my inner life and my behavior? One thing is for sure, my inner life and hence my entire being is affected by the people, the circumstances, and the situations that I confront and how I act and react to them. Communication with God should be a vital part of this formational process and if it is not, the void will be filled by conditioning elements far less desirable.

This chapter cannot conclude without addressing the work of the Holy Spirit. When an individual invites Jesus into His heart, it should be noted that the other members of the Trinity are not left standing outside. When Christ comes in, so too does the entire Trinity: Father, Son, and the Holy Spirit. As the Christian proceeds in daily discipleship and grows deeper in the faith, there comes a point where a deeper work of God's Spirit will be desired. At the consent of the saint of God, the Holy Spirit — already present in the life of the believer — is loosed to enter fully into every fiber, every nook and cranny of our beings. We loose the Spirit! And hence, we become "full of the Spirit." We allow Him, as far as we know how, to take control of our movements, our money, our sexuality . . . everything! And we find that we are indeed able to love God with all our heart, all our soul, all our strength. The disciple that truly wants to be all that he is meant to be, and do all that he is meant to do, will seek the "loosening" of God's Spirit in his life. God wants to come in, and He wants to fill. We should desire others to hold us accountable for such an infilling and overflowing.

C.S. Lewis, in *Prince Caspian,* masterfully portrays a discussion, after a time of separation, between the Savior-figure Aslan and the child Lucy.

> "Welcome, child," he said.
> "Aslan," said Lucy, "you're bigger."
> "That is because you are older, little one," answered he.
> "Not because you are?"
> "I am not. But every year you grow, you will find me bigger."[13]

A bigger God, not because He is, but because we are, makes a life of devotion worth pursuing—inside the prayer closet and out.

Bulletin Board

How often we put religion into a sacred day, Sunday, and a sacred place, the church, and leave it there — embalmed! (E. Stanley Jones)

In the past, it was necessary only for the Church to ring its bell for the people to come to it. Now, however, it is necessary for the Church to take the bell to the people. (Pope Paul VI)

Genuine holiness will find its expression in unrewarded service to the last, the least and the lost. (Frederick Coutts)

Some wish to live within the sound of church and chapel bell. I wish to run a rescue mission within a yard of hell. (C.T. Studd)

The world perceives us as pious and self-centered in our protected sanctuaries and multimillion-dollar church complexes — but that is simply not where most of the sick, hurting, and hungry people are, so they never hear our message. But imagine what would happen if the poor and needy could see us where *they* live, as we meet them at their point of need. (Charles Colson)

CHAPTER THREE

Mission

A story from India recalls the Brahman who attended an evangelistic meeting where Christians glowingly described how Christ had saved them. "You people say you are saved," declared the Brahman. "So am I. As Christ has saved you, so Krishna has saved me." The missionary in charge of the meeting replied, "I am very glad to hear that you are saved—very glad indeed. Now we are going down to the outcaste quarters and are going to see what we can do for these poor people. We will sit on their beds and in their houses and will share their lives to help them. Will you join us?" The Brahman thought a moment and then said, "Well, sahib, I am saved, but I am not saved that far."[1]

How saved are we? Enough to take the Gospel out of our meeting houses and into the lives of people who desperately need our Savior? Enough to escape our own agendas and schedules to put the Great Commission (Matt. 28:16-20) into action? Kublai Khan, in 1266, requested the Roman pope to "Send me 100 men skilled in your religion . . . and so I shall be baptized, and then all my barons and great men, and then their subjects. And so there will be more Christians here than in your parts." Two Dominicans were sent, but turned back. Twelve years later, the pope sent five others. *The Almanac of the Christian World* calls this the "greatest missed opportunity in Christian history."[2] I have to wonder how many opportunities I am missing by being more concerned with safety than Christian adventure.

Outward bound. That is the normative call for the Christian. When God told Abram to leave Haran and its resident moon god, He reiterated why the patriarch was being challenged with such a call. "I will bless you," says God. "And you will be a blessing. . . . all peoples on earth will be blessed through you" (Gen. 12:1-2). The call to today's churchfolk is no different. We have been blessed — not simply for the maintenance of our spiritual comfort (*inward* bound), but in order to be a blessing to all peoples in our world.

The insightful Archbishop of Canterbury, William Temple (1881–1944), described the church of Jesus Christ as the only cooperative society that exists for the benefit of its *non*members. The Gospel does not belong exclusively inside the four walls of the church, but:

> In the streets . . . where the message and practical aid of Christ can impact those who have not yet heard the Gospel news.

> In the streets . . . where it can touch the poor, the disinherited, the needy.

> In the streets . . . where secular Jane — who wouldn't dare lay foot inside an ecclesiastical structure — can see what an "in the flesh" Christian is really all about.

> In the streets . . . where the Gospel chroniclers tell us Christ was most of the time with His loving touch, His attempts to reach the lost, His voice that loved to tell the story.

Charles Colson reveals the Soviet government's shrewd legislative ploy in 1929 when, attempting to wipe out the church, a law was passed not to prevent people from meeting on Sunday morning but to make it a crime to conduct church school, to help the poor, to evangelize. "Stay in your churches on Sunday," said the officials, "and have church — period." The implicit assumption? If Christians obeyed the law at this point, the movement would die. Colson adds this stinger: "What the Soviet Communists did *by decree* in 1929, we are allowing to be done to us today *by default.*"[3] His analysis is, unfortunately, correct. The raw data of research indicates that American Christianity has opted out of missionary discipleship.

- No county in the U.S. has as great a percentage of its population attending church today as a decade ago.
- Between 80 percent and 85 percent of all churches in America are either plateaued or are declining.
- Edward Dayton reports that churches are losing 2,756,000 members per year to nominalism or unbelief.
- Up to 6,000 churches die every year for lack of a dream, lack of redemptive outreach, and lack of "beyond the four walls" activity.
- In the normal church 10 percent of the people do up to 90 percent of the work and 65 percent of the giving.
- David Barrett says in his *World Christian Encyclopedia* that Protestantism is shrinking from two-thirds of the population in 1900 to one-third by the year 2000.[4]

We need to be held accountable for our activity and our inactivity, our giving and our keeping! One thing is for sure, a maintenance-plagued organization is not the church as Christ meant for it to be; not holiness the way God intended for His people to reflect Him; not "blessed to be a blessing," the destiny God desires for His "chosen people." We need a modern-day concept of discipleship reflective of the biblical mandate. When we are called to Christ, we are called to follow Him. And His footsteps will lead us to the places of need in our communities, in our nations, in the world.

20/20 Vision
One of my friends recently preached a message at our seminary chapel using the metaphor of an eye chart. Eye charts, as you remember, have either a series of letters which the examinee attempts to identify or an "E" pointing in various directions. But, said my friend, imagine an eye chart with a cross on it. The disciples, lacking the proper focus, keep looking at the chart and offering seemingly absurd interpretations: "I see a throne," a couple of them admit. "I spy an easy chair," say others. On another occasion they see a country club and on still another, an Oval Office. But they never see the cross. They never see the hardship, the pain, the sweat. They need vision correction!
Sid McCollum hit the nail on the head when he said:

Let's face it — 99 percent of us (maybe more) are scared silly of the word MISSIONS. We really like the idea of someone "forsaking all for Christ and the Gospel" — as long as that someone is someone else. . . .

What's our problem? In a nutshell, it's this: we see the world differently than God does. We haven't quite caught His plan, His vision, His hope for this world. And until we do, we'll never fully understand what our role can be in the challenge set before us.

Missionary Christianity is seeing things the way God sees them! And that means that we will invest our lives meeting needs when we see things that break the heart of God. That may mean going halfway around the world to spend the rest of our lives. Sometimes God's nudge will send us across the street, to minister in ways only a neighbor can. Whatever else, it will mean that we *go*, wherever God wants, to be His angels in a world that needs His touch.

Out of the Fortress
In Frank Tillapaugh's important volume, *Unleashing the Church*, he contrasts the church as it has too often become — a fortress — and the church as it was meant to be — unleashed.

The fortress church puts up its building, starts its programs and concentrates primarily within its walls. The church unleashed is not unconcerned with what goes on within its church buildings, but it is only partially focused there. In the church unleashed an individual's primary ministry may be within one of many traditional church programs such as Sunday School. But there is an equal chance that his ministry may be in a prison or working with a foreign student. In either case, the norm is people-oriented ministry.[5]

Early in his book, Tillapaugh notes the difference between two meetings he attended, one of a parachurch organization and the other, a regional denominational gathering. The parachurch meeting was marked by excitement and anticipation. Their passion was evident as area directors reported growth in conversions, staffs, training centers, evangelistic activities. These people were clearly convinced that their world could be won for Christ. A short time later, Tillapaugh observed the denominational gathering. There, instead of, "How can we win our world for Christ?" the question was, "How can we hang on for another year?"

Tillapaugh challenges us to an experiment:

> Ask church people what they think of when you mention the church and its ministries. The vast majority of answers will fall within a very narrow range including, preaching, Sunday School, choir, children's and ladies' auxiliaries and youth programs. Don't anticipate answers such as street people, ex-convicts, prisoners, sailors, unchurched high school kids or members of the cults. . . . When Dawson Trotman wanted to reach sailors, he realized the church was hopelessly turned inward. So he bypassed it.[6]

Tillapaugh's church, Bear Valley Baptist, has decided that the best way to structure for ministry is to scrap standing committees for the most part and allow the emergence of small groups focused on needs. These groups dream ministry dreams and say "Yes, we will do it" not "Yes, we should do it." Mere committees are radically transformed into ministry groups committed to getting the job done! Church of the Savior in Washington, D.C. has a similar setup. When any member feels led to establish a new ministry he "sounds the call." At the conclusion of a worship service the vision is shared by the individual(s), and all who are interested in "testing the call" come forward and probe the issue through inquiry and prayer. The idea might be tabled for the time being, or others in the room might feel drawn toward the vision and begin to set in motion a ministry.

Evangelism
Dr. Win Arn compiled some startling statistics about America early in 1987.

There are 96 million Americans with no religious affiliation, 73 million Christians in name only which make up 169 million or 71 percent of the population. Only five other countries in the world have a population larger than 169 million. America is a legitimate mission field.

Protestantism in America has shrunk from a two thirds proportion in 1900 to what will be a one third proportion by the end of the century.

No county in the U.S. has a greater percentage of its population attending church today than it did a decade ago.

In 1900 there were 27 churches for every 10,000 Americans. In 1950 there were 17 churches for every 10,000 Americans. In 1985 there were 12 churches for every 10,000 Americans.

Black Americans are only 30 percent evangelized. Black Africans are 50 percent evangelized.[7]

No question about it, America is a sizable mission field for which Christians are responsible. And it can be profoundly affected for Christ if significant numbers of us allow others to hold us accountable for personal involvement in such evangelization.

According to church growth experts, the best way to reach any mission field is not through polished programs or flashy media, but through personal relationships. The people most effective at reaching the lost are not big-name evangelists or fast-talking door-to-door pitchmen, but (are you ready for this?) normal church people like you and me who have unchurched Friends, Relatives, Associates, and Neighbors (FRANs).

Research shows that each church member has, on the average, about 6–8 unchurched FRANs. This means, essentially, that if your church is 100 people strong today your potential congregation is 600–800! Those 600–800 FRANs, the church growth pundits remind us, are the most receptive of any with whom your church will come into contact. Church leadership ought to emphasize this often overlooked strategy by building bridges of care and loving concern to these folks and basing programs on their felt needs. Encouragement to reach out in love and accountability for seeing that strategy through, should be linchpins of our local efforts. Churches who take this principle of "frangelism" to heart grow, and research shows that the more seriously the approach is taken, the more people are brought to know Christ as their Savior.

We *should* be held accountable to love and meet the needs of our friends, relatives, associates, and neighbors, and over the bridge of that care and concern bring those people into our churches and, of course, to God.

Social Action
Evangelism and social action are, in many respects, two sides of the same coin. They are both good news, and we should engage in both. Stanley Jones often said that evangelism without social action was a body without a soul. Social action without evangelism was like a soul without a body. "One is a ghost," said Jones, "and the other a corpse. We don't want either one!"

Tony Campolo, the consummate storyteller, recalls a dining experience in Haiti. The waiter seated Campolo's party next to a large window before taking his order and bringing a scrumptious dinner of steak and all the trimmings. About the time Campolo took his first bite, he looked to his left where a small crowd of Haitian children had their noses pressed up against the glass, staring at the food on his plate. Campolo put down his fork, unable to eat. The waiter, obviously used to the scenario, closed the venetian blind. "Enjoy your meal," said the man. "Don't let them bother you." Campolo's thought, in retrospect: "Isn't that what we all do? Pull down the blinds so that we don't have to see the suffering peoples of the earth?"[8]

We have good news to share. The best-case scenario is that those we minister to will want the new life in Christ that we proclaim. Some will take only our bread—or whatever we offer to meet their felt need—and leave physically full. But real evangelism is reaching out to meet needs in the name of Jesus whether those needs are physical, emotional, or spiritual. Sometimes the response is positive and because of met needs, people commit themselves to the God we proclaim. But, as even Jesus found, not always. Nonetheless, our calling is clear. Below are a few hands-on alternatives for personal or group involvement in your own community:

- Ministry to the elderly such as the many outreach programs to shut-ins, adopt a grandparent, regular programs at nursing homes.
- Housing for the poor (e.g., Habitat for Humanity)
- Soup kitchens/Rescue missions
- Ministry to the handicapped (mental, physical, emotional)
- Big Brothers/Big Sisters
- Prison ministry
- Long- or short-term overseas missions
- Political lobbying for biblical priorities
- Pro-life activity
- Outreach to unwed mothers
- Addictions ministry (alcohol, drugs, etc.)
- Ministry to AIDS patients
- Literacy
- Reaching out to felt needs of poor in your community
- Inner city ministry

Good-bye 9 to 5

Many of us need to begin investigating creative ways to release ourselves from normal avenues of employment in order to invest more time in service. To do so is neither easy nor expedient—and is frequently sacrificial. But the stories of those who follow this path are inspiring.

John Steinbeck once described people who suffer poverty, oppression, and unending adversity in this life. "And when they died," he penned, "it was as though they never lived." My next-door neighbor, Jim Young, would read those words and think of the elderly of Jackson, Mississippi. Jim was reputed by many in this city, and across the state, to be one of the finest newspapermen in the region. According to an editor at the local paper, "Jim was certainly one of the top journalists in the state and had more influence over public policy than even some government officials." But as he observed the difficulties faced by old people with little or no family and dwindling resources, Jim yearned to devote himself full-time to a ministry that would enhance their lives. His next step surprised everyone. He quit his job and began to investigate possibilities for service. Through the dreams of Jim and his church, a ministry to the elderly has been established. It hasn't come without some frustration, without significant lifestyle changes and a few questions for God along the way. Jim has been offered prestigious positions, but he and his wife Michelle feel that they are where God wants them. A growing number of Jackson's elderly agree.

Cathy Dudley grew up in Appalachia on the "wrong side of town." Her life of poverty took a different turn, however, when she married someone from the "other side of town" and moved to Dallas. There she spent the bulk of her time raising two children while her husband established an extremely successful business. After accepting Christ, she began opening her home to needy people. Her husband joked that every time she went to the grocery store she brought home someone else—a person on the verge of suicide, a prostitute, a transient. The Dudley home soon became a hospital for those in need of healing.

As their family matured, the situation was less beneficial for school-age children who needed their home to be more of a refuge. So Cathy sought God's guidance. Mindful of her frustration and hopelessness during early years of poverty, she began through prayer and Bible study to formulate a plan. Scripture repeatedly reminded her of God's concern for the disenfranchised. With her children in school and her husband's business thriving, she had daytime hours free for service.

She began to hear more and more about West Dallas, an impoverished area of which she had heretofore been ignorant. To learn about inner-city ministry she contacted "Voice of Calvary," an outreach in Jackson, Mississippi. Armed with the support of the Jackson-based organization, she set up an organization in West Dallas called "Voice of Hope." Today Voice of Hope has a four-faceted ministry of (1) outreach to children and youth consisting of Bible Clubs, job/skills training and leadership development; (2) adult and family ministries including adult literacy courses, financial counseling, and educational projects; (3) senior citizens ministry which includes Bible classes, shut-in visitation by nurses, arts and crafts; and (4) family ministries spanning all age-groups and providing a health club which offers such activities as aerobics, nutrition counseling, dental and eye clinics, and education services and special projects like the recent "West Dallas Clean-up" involving over 375 people who pitched in to spruce up their environment. There is also a Christmas store that redistributes toys and clothes at a third of the retail price so that West Dallas parents and senior citizens can shop affordably. Called to minister to the whole community, Cathy and her colleagues seek to use Christian principles of self-help, evangelism, and renewal to raise up Christian leaders in West Dallas.

We've looked at Jim Young and Cathy Dudley, but the list of examples could go on for pages . . . the plumber who works hard four days a week to pay for the "plain necessaries of life" (as Wesley put it) in order to make the rest of the week available for evangelism . . . the teacher who spreads her nine-month salary over twelve in order to have three "paid for" months each summer to serve the poor and disen-franchised in her city . . . the couple who saved enough to retire early, and headed to South America to support them-selves in mission work . . . the homemaker who spends ten hours each week lobbying the state legislature for pro-family issues.

The key in each of these examples, however, is persons willing to renounce the assumption that more money, more leisure, or a better position was their obvious calling. They recognized their particular gifts and made a sacrifice to ex-tend those gifts to a needy world. They asked strange ques-tions, like: "What is God doing today in this world and how can I help?" or, "If God could have His way with this commu-nity, this people, this neighborhood, what would happen? What can I do about it?" They ponder issues that make al-most no sense to our world, such as: "Why settle for more and miss the best?" And they ask, knowing they are part of God's answer. They hear His pronouncement to His people, "Blessed to be a blessing," and really believe that they are.

Is there a way you could simplify your lifestyle and reduce your expenditures to free up some time and energy for God's work in your community? Can you and a team of people find a way to effectively evangelize the lost, feed the hungry, or comfort the afflicted? What could God do with your gifts if applied to a needy situation ten or more hours a week? One Sunday School class in urban Seattle was challenged by its teacher to design an imaginative way to address the compelling human need in that city. The catch: invent a way to work twenty hours a week to support thirty hours of weekly ministry.

The opportunities are endless! Talk to God, read your Bible, get some counsel from your small group, dream some dreams, free up some time, and go.

Sanctifying Your Vocation

"Vocation," says Walter Brueggemann, "is finding a purpose for being in the world that is related to the purposes of God."[9] Considering the hours in each day and the energy and time we devote to jobs, shouldn't we tie in our vocational calling with the work of God in the world?

Tom Sine debunks the "myth of penetrationist thinking." Penetrationist thinking goes something like this: "What the world really needs are laypeople who are willing to take their Christian commitment with them into the workplace—into the law offices, into the schools, into the factories, into the highways and byways of *real* life." Nice idealism, says Sine. It's just that most of the time the ideal is myth. The familiar line, "Whatever job you work at is automatically your Christian vocation," usually ends up as justification for a line of work that never allows the participant to effect kingdom breakthroughs in society. It is not impossible; it simply rarely happens. Sine, in *Why Settle for More and Miss the Best?* poses these prophetic questions:

> Where does one find biblical support for the view that one's job automatically becomes one's Christian vocation? Where is the scriptural support for the view that every job is as good as every other job?
>
> Does a job doing advertising for the tobacco industry or producing compounds for our chemical warfare stockpiles rank as a Christian vocation? Isn't it true that some jobs are actually counter-kingdom? And aren't there jobs

in which employees spend large amounts of time and energy creating products or services that are essentially useless or unnecessary?

... Remember, Christ's earliest followers quit jobs that provided fish for the homes of Galilee in order to invest their working hours more intentionally in the advance of God's kingdom, which was radically challenging the existing society. The consequence of the "anything you do is your vocation" model is that we wind up with a lot of Christians doing more to maintain the status quo in a fallen world than they are doing to advance the cause of God's kingdom. In my opinion, that is not what God has in mind when He calls us to take part in His Story.[10]

In the movie *Superman* there is a scene where Clark Kent is upset and frustrated after a football game in which he was reduced to being a manager. He possesses supernatural powers yet must hide them from peers who don't accept him because he is not a star, only a team manager. Kent's father slips an arm around the soon-to-be "Superman" and says, "Son, you are here for a special reason. I don't know what that reason is—but I know one thing—it's not to score touchdowns."

Called for a reason—special, talented, sent to earth for some cause—but "not to score touchdowns." That has caused me to think. I believe that more and more of us who accept God's offer of salvation should investigate our deeper reason for being. Ask what God is doing in the world today and discover a way to either find a job that fits His purposes, or remold our present jobs into avenues for redemptive activity. When we become truly Christian, we should be held accountable for wrestling with such crucial issues and coming to conclusions that maximize our lives for His kingdom.

Should we run out and find new jobs if we are having difficulty seeing God work through our jobs at the Coca-Cola bottling factory or punching keys at IBM? Well, I think it highly possible that God would ask you to leave to fully invest your life and time in His kingdom. But suppose you become convinced God would have you choose that job and

"penetrate" that workplace for Him? Keep in mind that you
will undoubtedly need these four things:
- a vocation that is by clear evidence in your life a "God-
  calling," transcending career success, the achievement of
  higher position, and more money.
- a tenacious attitude that you *will*, by God's grace, have a
  strategic and profound impact upon your workplace and
  society for God's kingdom purposes.
- an accountability support team to undergird your kingdom endeavors in the workplace.
- continual reevaluation to be sure you are where God
  wants you and you are having the kind of impact on
  society that He has called you to have.

It is highly possible that John Doe, businessman, can have
a powerful impact where he works. John can catch a vision of
his business as a chance to share Christ with the unevan-
gelized both within and without the institution. He can work
to structure his organization according to Christian principles.
He can seek ways for his product and the profits from his
work to serve evangelistic ends. He can investigate possibilities for support group Bible studies. He can use his vocation,
in essence, as a conduit for God's activity in the world! Opportunities abound within many jobs if we look to God for
inspiration.

A Bit Frightened?
The Russian Aleksandr Solzhenitsyn, at a Harvard com-
mencement in the late 1970s, declared, "Even biology knows
that extreme safety and well-being are not advantageous for a
living organism." It is a bit daunting to be asked to leave the
fortress and enter the world with our message. But moving
beyond ourselves is healthy for individuals, groups, churches,
or nations. Safety and well-being are not our calling. Being
outward bound and loving people as much as Jesus loves us,
are. Forward march!

Bulletin Board

The minimum responsibility for any Christian in the area of finances is that he share economic secrets with his brothers and sisters. (Art Gish)

Money. 200 proof. Taken straight or mixed with many lovely things, it's the most intoxicating substance known to man. (David Augsburger)

If a man's religion does not affect his use of money, that man's religion is in vain. (Hugh Martin)

I believe that God is the total owner of my life and resources. I give God the throne in relation to the material aspect of my life. God is the owner, I am the ower. Because God is a lavish giver, I too shall be lavish and cheerful in my regular gifts. (Members' Covenant of the Church of the Savior—Washington, D.C.)

There are three conversions necessary: the conversion of the heart, mind, and the purse. (Martin Luther)

CHAPTER FOUR
Money

There are probably many ways to seek an objective evaluation of a person's spirituality. In quest of some innovative approaches, I decided one day to ask a group of my students which part of a person's life they would examine in order to gauge the health of his spiritual life. "It may sound simplistic," said one of my students, "but I would begin by seeing how many times they go to church in a year." "Do they pray and read their Bible?" said another. "That's always a good 'acid test.' " Another hand shot up. "I can always tell if someone is 'spiritual' — so to speak — if they are not frightened to talk about their Christian commitment before their non-Christian friends." One student wanted to delve into the family. "Let me see how that man or woman treats his or her spouse and you'll have some real clues!"

Perhaps such answers could give an indication of modern-day spirituality. But if you were a member of the investigative team assigned to make an accurate assessment about a person's commitment to God with just one piece of evidence, I would recommend to you the personal checkbook. My guess is that that piece of evidence is one of the most objective tests about us and one of the most telling as regarding our spiritual health, our priorities, dreams, and addictions. Ron Blue, financial expert, agrees:

A life story could be written from a checkbook. It reflects your goals, priorities, convictions, relationships, and even the use of your time. A person who has been a Christian for even a short while can fake prayer, Bible study, evangelism, going to church, and so on, but he can't fake what his checkbook reveals.[1]

I don't want to overstate the case because only God's gracious hand can save, but it is probably true that the checkbook is one of the best measures of how much we have allowed that grace to impact our lives. And it is here that we are in desperate need of practical guidelines. Many of us have yet to learn what a personal budget governed by biblical priorities looks like. Blue reminds us of this sad truth, noting that "Christians are no better money managers than non-Christians."[2]

Helpful accountability and practical advice are needed now. Probably no area of our lives requires more loving confrontation than that of how our balance sheet squares with the work of the Lord in this world.

The Big Secret

Like many other Christian pilgrims, I have found almost everything easier to discuss with others than my own personal finances. At least initially. But once we get over our timidity about having God and His church struggle with us in this vital area, we will find it is genuinely beneficial to seek counsel regarding financial decisions.

These words from the pen of Doris Janzen Longacre lay bare our common attitude, however, concerning personal finances.

> You and he belong to the same body of Christ in this town. Today you sit together in the pew, sharing a hymnbook: "Take my life and let it be consecrated, Lord, to Thee."
>
> This morning your hands met in greeting and while passing the offering plate and Communion tray. You're on the same committee and in the same weekly prayer group. Your families often call a short-notice picnic. You offer casseroles when they're sick and they feed your dogs when you go on vacation. You phoned them first when your last baby was born and they you when their grandmother died. Last year you even spent Christmas Eve together. Best friends. And in the Lord.
>
> But still, you keep The Secret. . . .
>
> Money. How much does each have and what do they

do with it? We have our stewardship drives and our poster thermometers for special projects. But seldom does anyone divulge to a sister or brother in the church the specific information needed to receive counsel in handling what 1 Timothy 6:10 calls "the root of all evil." The scarcity of testimonies which express freedom between Christians guiding each other on money's use suggests hard tasks ahead for the church.[3]

Accountability and helpful interpersonal relationships do not necessarily entail waving our budgets for approval before a wide assembly of people—even if they are churchfolk. I'll not dismiss the possibility that there may be a time for that. But generally speaking, a small group of intimate believers may be able to help us understand the biblical imperative for our finances and gently guide us to adjust our priorities not only for the sake of our families, but also the families of the world. For most of us who have grown used to "The Secret," interpersonal divulsion alone will be challenging. But it may also be one of the most liberating exercises that we can undertake. Before we talk about the accountability aspect of financial matters, however, let's take a brief look at the biblical view of money and how it relates to our spiritual lives.

Lessons from the Old Testament
The lessons on this topic from Scripture are many. For instance, the Bible says five times more about money than the vitally important subject of prayer. There are 500 plus verses on such things as prayer and faith but over 2,000 verses dealing with money and possessions.[4] It doesn't take an astute biblical scholar to recognize that God was aggressively using repetition in order to teach His people about the relationship between money, possessions, and spirituality.

The starting point for our discussion begins, as did God's instruction on the matter, in Old Testament history. While not belaboring any single text or portion of Scripture, let us take note that through events and people, God communicated to the nation of Israel His principles for the use of possessions and money. Though certainly far from exhaustive, this sampling will hopefully be informative.

The Garden of Eden narrative (Gen. 1–3)

It was in the Garden that good material initially gave way through poor choice to materialism as man and woman chose to obey their desires rather than God. Whenever you put -ism on the end of a word it connotes devotion. Devotion is good, if directed toward the right thing or person. In Eden, however, it seems that instead of there being a proper allegiance to God, materialism elevated desire above obedience. Adam and Eve hid from God — a common reaction when we have followed our own appetites at the expense of God's plan for us. Whatever can be said about materialism, however, God made the material good ("God saw all that He had made, and it was very good" [Gen. 1:31]). That should help us keep a wholesome view of God's goodness and His call to us, as the climax of His creation, to enjoy that goodness. His intention is that the community of God delight in and benefit from His handiwork.

The call and life of Abraham (Gen. 12ff)

The life of Abraham has much to teach about God's economic desire for us. It pinpoints, in many ways, the lavish generosity of God and His provision for His people. God calls Abram from his homeland to make His name great (contrast this with the people in 11:4ff who want to make their own names great). When God calls and man follows, God will provide. In the story of Abram, this included material matters as well as other ways. As the lesson was passed on to the nation of Israel, such blessing was contingent on the human response of obedience.

As Richard Foster indicates:

> We do need to stress that the promise of material blessing was a conditioned promise. It was no blank check. There was the stipulation, "If you are willing and obedient you shall eat the good of the land" (Isa. 1:19). That is to say, there was the strong emphasis upon the inward nature of simplicity — holy obedience — that conditioned all the promised provision. And a vital aspect of that obedience was compassionate provision for the poor and needy.[5]

The Year of Jubilee (Lev. 25)

Once every fifty years God intended that Israel return all land to its original owners. Not only that, but at the sound of the trumpet on the Day of Atonement, all debts were to be canceled and all slaves set free. Evidently God was trying to instill in the people the principle that He was the Owner of the land (Lev. 25:23) and that they were only given use of it. The purchaser of property was buying the harvests, not the land itself—for it was not a person's to buy or sell! The acquisitiveness of the rich was held in check, and no longer was a downward spiral of poverty the inevitable heritage of the poor. If you had to sell yourself into slavery in order to get out of debt, you and your children would eventually get a new start. No longer could debt just add up because of apparent misfortune. Eventually you would be free! Says Ron Sider, "That this passage prescribes justice rather than haphazard handouts by wealthy philanthropists is extremely significant. . . . It is to be the poor person's right to receive back his inheritance at the time of Jubilee. Returning the land is not a charitable courtesy that the wealthy may extend if they please."[6]

Laws on tithing and firstfruits

The first production of grain, wine, oil, or produce was to be brought to the sanctuary for presentation as firstfruits (Deut. 26:1-11).[7] Again, through God's legal system He was teaching that the first belongs to Him. The Israelites were not to wait until it was convenient but in trust and faith give immediately from the results of their hard labor and expect God to continue to bless.

The tithe was first practiced by Abraham after his defeat of Kedorlaomer and the kings who were with him (Gen. 14:17-24). Melchizedek, King of Salem, greeted Abraham upon his arrival and Abraham lavishly gave him a tenth of the spoils. The King of Sodom then received the rest. This spirit of joy in giving was handed on in Mosaic Law. In Deuteronomy God commanded Israel to tithe, but I have rarely heard these verses cited by pastors trying to increase giving.

You shall surely tithe. . . . And you shall eat in the presence of the Lord your God, at the place where He chooses to establish His name. . . . And you may spend the money for whatever your heart desires, for oxen, or sheep, or wine, or strong drink, or whatever your heart desires; and there you shall eat in the presence of the Lord your God and rejoice, you and your household. Also you shall not neglect the Levite who is in your town, for he has no portion or inheritance among you (14:22-27, NASB).

Of course, the most familiar text for tithe sermons comes from Malachi 3:8-12. There, God says that it is possible to rob Him by not giving tithes and offerings as the people had been commanded. Give, and they would be blessed. Withhold, and they would be judged. He told Israel to "bring the whole tithe into the storehouse." Larry Burkett explains the purpose of the storehouse in ancient Israel.

A storehouse in the Old Testament had four functions: 1) It was used to feed the tribe of Levi and the priests of Aaron. . . . 2) It was used to feed the prophets. . . . 3) It was used to feed the Hebrew widows and orphans living within the city. . . . 4) It was used to feed the widows and orphans of the Gentiles, living in and around the Hebrew city. A special tithe was taken every third year to do this.[8]

Burkett emphasizes that many churches in America do this kind of thing, and many do not. "If a local church doesn't accept the responsibility of being the storehouse, then believers must ensure that the fourfold function is accomplished through other means." Burkett also points out another interesting nuance of the Scripture. He identifies three tithes described in the Old Testament—two given each year and an additional tithe every third year—that average out to 23⅓ percent annually. This is not even speaking of the extra offerings that were quite regular. Those who desire to be literal about the tithe of the Old Testament might have to transcend the relatively easy "10-percent challenge" that most churches request of their parishioners![9]

Watered-down tithe messages that try to squeeze a 10-percent commitment out of church folk have done much to hurt the kingdom. The song "All to Jesus, I Surrender" has been rendered "10 percent I give to Jesus, 10 percent I freely give" in many of our sermons. God asks for much more than that, as we will eventually demonstrate.

The destruction of Sodom and Gomorrah (Ezek. 16:49)
One of the most overlooked but crucial passages in the Old Testament is this one tucked away in Ezekiel.

> Behold, this was the guilt of your sister Sodom: she and her daughters had arrogance, abundant food, and careless ease, but she did not help the poor and needy. Thus they were haughty and committed abominations before Me. Therefore I removed them when I saw it (Ezek. 16:49, NASB).

Like many, before I happened on to this verse, I had assumed sexual perversion alone was the downfall of Sodom. And certainly, that played a part. But a lack of concern for a group of people so very important in God's economy—the poor—contributed significantly to spiritual destruction.

The prophets' messages to Israel and Judah (cf. Amos 5:11-15; Isa. 58:3-7; Jer. 5:26-29; 7:5-7)
God's message thunders down to His people: worship without economic justice is evil; I demand provision for the orphan, the widow, and the poor; I will judge—harshly—those nations who do not obey My commands regarding the oppressed and needy; finally, I will bless those who amend their ways and deeds for the sake of economic justice and righteousness.

Again, these are just some of the verses that appear in the Old Testament. But they are crucial ones, reflecting God's priorities for the use of money and possessions.

Lessons from the New Testament
"Do not think that I came to abolish the Law or the Prophets," said Jesus. "I did not come to abolish, but to fulfill"

(Matt. 5:17, NASB). Jesus' words carry with them an important lesson. The Old Testament is indispensable to understanding the entire revelation of Scripture. As to money and possessions, the lessons of the Old Testament are not done away with but "built upon" — fulfilled — in the New Testament instruction on this vital subject.

Lessons from Jesus

Jesus talks about money. Quite a bit, in fact. The topic is on His lips more than any other with the exception of the kingdom of God.[10] In fact, according to Howard I. Dayton, Jr., sixteen out of thirty-eight of Christ's parables deal with money. In all, over one out of ten Gospel verses directly addresses our finances.[11] As in the Old Testament, the subject of money and possessions was too important not to talk about — and frequently!

Jesus did not mince words. He spoke boldly and with authority, forcefully driving home His points. He knew, as the witness of the entire biblical account attests, that wealth has unusual and frequently destructive power. It tempts us to place our faith in things instead of God, fosters less compassion for the poor and stunts healthy spirituality. But Jesus was no ascetic. He Himself did not come from the poor class of Jews but from a family of carpenters. He occasionally fellowshipped with the wealthy and even picked up some well-heeled disciples along the way (Nicodemus, Joseph of Arimathea). By virtue of His ethnic identity He undoubtedly took part in many joyous Jewish celebrations, including weddings, where at one juncture He even provided the drinks.

Following are three principles that must carry forward to our day:

- Jesus criticized wealth and notes at every point the danger of possessions. Although they are not evil in themselves, the place that they frequently take in our hearts is, and we must guard ourselves diligently.
- Material is good; materialism is bad. Jesus was not an ascetic and didn't call us to asceticism either. As Augustine reminds us, created material is like a ring from the Beloved, but only a ring. Material goods themselves are not the Beloved. Ron Sider points out, "Sometimes par-

ticular circumstances — such as an urgent mission or the needs of the poor — may require their renunciation." Nonetheless, the elements of God's creation are still gifts from Him and signs of His love. They are wonderful blessings if we keep that perspective. When we mistake them for the Beloved, as is a frequent temptation, it is to our detriment.[12]

● Wealth, used aright, is a glorious means of grace. Personal needs should be provided; God's ministry in the world should increase; the poor should be cared for; godly celebration should be constant.

It is obviously no mistake that the great Christian saints and communities in the years following Jesus' ascension adopted these principles as an economic formula toward dynamic character and service in the kingdom of God. This we begin to see in the early church of the Book of Acts.

The early church

When the Spirit of God fell at Pentecost it must have been a sight to behold — for many reasons, not the least being the economic miracles that began taking place within the fellowship of believers.

Everyone was filled with awe. . . . All the believers were together and had everything in common. Selling their possessions and goods, they gave to anyone as he had need (Acts 2:42-45).

All the believers were one in heart and mind. No one claimed that any of his possessions was his own, but they shared everything they had. . . . There were no needy persons among them. For from time to time those who owned lands or houses sold them, brought the money from the sales and put it at the apostles' feet, and it was distributed to anyone as he had need (4:32-35).

As noted earlier from Scripture, when people are obedient to what God ordains, blessing follows. Thus the Jerusalem church was adding to its number those who were being saved, people were praising God, and believers were of one heart and mind as "much grace was with them all" (v. 33). But isn't it interesting that in the next few verses the Ananias and Sapphira story appears. A couple is deceptive with their funds and, as a result, both husband and wife fall down dead. In the first recorded sin in the life of the church, God's divine judgment reveals how seriously He takes money matters. At few places in Scripture are joyous giving and dishonesty, and God's clear reaction to them both, placed so close together.

Among other lessons in the New Testament, perhaps the most telling are the requirements for righteous Christian living and the disqualifications for leadership found in Paul's writings:

Now the overseer must be . . . not a lover of money (1 Tim. 3:2-3).

Deacons are to be men worthy of respect, sincere . . . not pursuing dishonest gain (v. 8).

Command those who are rich in this present world not to be arrogant nor to put their hope in wealth, which is so uncertain, but to put their hope in God (6:17).

But godliness with contentment is great gain. For we brought nothing into the world, and we can take nothing out of it. But if we have food and clothing, we will be content with that. People who want to get rich fall into temptation and a trap and into many foolish and harmful desires that plunge men into ruin and destruction. For the love of money is a root of all kinds of evil. Some people, eager for money, have wandered from the faith and pierced themselves with many griefs (vv. 6-10).

For of this you can be sure: No immoral, impure or greedy person—such a man is an idolater—has any inheritance in the kingdom of Christ and of God (Eph. 5:5).

But now I am writing you that you must not associate with anyone who calls himself a brother but is sexually immoral or greedy. . . . With such a man do not even eat (1 Cor. 5:11).

And now brothers, we want you to know about the grace that God has given the Macedonian churches. Out of the most severe trial, their overflowing joy and their extreme poverty well up in rich generosity. For I testify that they gave as much as they were able, and even beyond their ability (2 Cor. 8:1-3).

Of course, the New Testament frequently addresses money. A study of James reveals several bold statements, including this one from the fifth chapter: "Now listen, you rich people, weep and wail because of the misery that is coming upon you" (5:1ff). The writer of Hebrews admonished the people to "keep your lives free from the love of money" (13:5). Scripture sets a clear direction for the church of the first and succeeding centuries and makes one thing plain — money is to be handled very carefully indeed. When we get some — and we all do — we need to be mindful of the biblical injunctions and prepare to spend and give wisely.

The Budget Process

It is important that every Christian have a budget. A twenty-five-year-old making $30,000 a year until his retirement at sixty-five will have earned $1.2 million in his lifetime. This projection assumes, of course, no cost of living increases or pay raises. The amount is surprisingly large and represents a substantial stewardship opportunity. At the point of that realization we begin to fathom the responsibility the Lord has given each of us for making and using money. Our mission is to use the funds in our care in a Christian manner that maximizes our influence for the kingdom of God. To accomplish this task we must know precisely how much money we amass during a week, month, or year, and where the Lord would have us place that money as responsible Christians in our global society. The guidance of people who love us, who have a world vision for Christ, and who have dealt with budget priorities from a Christian perspective will aid immeasurably in our task.

A simple dictionary definition identifies a budget as "adjusting expenses with income." It is, according to Larry Burkett,

> Nothing more than a short-range plan for how you will spend your money during the coming year.
>
> A budget should not restrict your freedom to enjoy life; it should expand it. "How," you say, "can living on a budget expand my freedom?" By helping you live within your means and not go into debt. If you're already in debt, a budget will help you out of it. A budget is not magical, and living on one won't permit you to spend more than you make and avoid debt. But a budget will tell you when you have spent all you can afford to each month in each category, such as entertainment, food, and gasoline. A budget also tells you how much you must save each month for one-time annual expenses, such as car insurance, property taxes, and clothing.[13]

I remember the first budget my wife and I used as a young couple. Knowing that we had to get a grip on our finances and feeling a little less than disciplined enough to make it work, we decided to give ourselves a visual reminder that when the money is gone, you can't spend it! Our plan was simple. Designate a portion of our monthly income for a number of categories and place that cash (and I mean cash!) in empty peanut-butter jars beneath the kitchen sink. After writing checks for church giving and rent we then designated money for such categories as food, clothing, entertainment, utilities, and insurance, and wadded the bills and change in our glass containers. When the peanut butter jars were empty — no more spending in that category. The intended lesson: you can't spend what you can't see (a lesson that our debtor nation has encouraged us to forget!). It was a harsh but very real and visible reminder! No credit cards, no tabs, no "charging." Believe me when I say that it took some radical restructuring of minds, hearts, and habits.

Our goal, not accomplished immediately, was to get

through the month without robbing another jar when one was empty and we still wanted to spend in that category. As a young couple without children one of those ever-encroaching categories was "entertainment." At the beginning of every month I would ask myself, "Do I *really* think we can make it on forty bucks of personal spending money in the next thirty days?" The answer: "No, I don't really believe it" and it really didn't happen much of the time. But our jars were a beginning. Eventually we learned that "robbing jars" for purposes outside that category would only hurt us down the line somewhere. The month that we needed our car engine worked on, for instance. Too many trips to the theater made that month rough. There is a pithy expression that began to embody for us some real-life philosophy: "Unhappiness is the result of sacrificing what we really want for what we want at the moment." What is it we wanted "at the moment"? To spend freely. What did we "really want"? Financial integrity after the biblical pattern and a balanced budget. It takes some practice!

A year with that peanut-butter-jar budget taught us that with discipline and honest effort budgets can work and are, as Burkett notes, liberating. For the first time we knew where our money was going, where we needed to spend less, and what new categories to develop to enhance our own accounting, and how to plan for future needs. By the way, don't keep glass jars underneath the sink unless that kind of visible reminder is absolutely necessary. First of all, it is not very secure from robbery or break-in. Second you may find, as my wife and I did, that your financial plan will be received by your friends with howls of laughter. But it helped us then, and laid the foundation for our family finances today. At some juncture we graduated to slightly revised categories and used envelopes instead of jars. Eventually, with the discipline in place, we moved to the use of a budget sheet and our checkbook to help us keep track. Mary and I still struggle, but the struggles inherent in the budgeting process are less difficult than living without one. We have found the planning more than worth it.

At the end of this chapter is a budget sheet similar to the one that we have used in past years. There is nothing particularly sacred about this plan. It merely contains a number of categories that have helped us sort out our priorities. Included at the bottom of the page is a place to put some goals and plans for the future. You might consider increased giving for such things as church offering, world hunger, missionary support, etc. Another worthwhile consideration is savings goals for the future. Definitely include debt reduction, if that is necessary in your situation. Use specific and achievable numbers and realistic target dates. Remember the fundamental question: How can I maximize my funds for the kingdom of God? That question, along with prayer and honest dialogue, should guide you through the process.

The Help of a Group

John was a close friend and a cycling enthusiast. We spent a lot of time together, and it wasn't long before his love of biking began to rub off on me. We flipped through magazines together, watched cycling events on TV, and discussed the sport on an almost daily basis. While John could occasionally borrow a bike for me from one of his friends, it wasn't long before I decided I needed to purchase my own. As my enthusiasm grew, we made frequent visits to area bike shops to inspect some of the latest models. The day finally came when I excitedly said to John, "It's time. Let's buy one!" John's advice was appropriate. "Matt, wouldn't it be a better idea to buy a used bike for now, instead of a $500 new one? That way, you can see if you'll really stick with the sport for several months or a year before splurging and buying something too expensive."

His observation was good and immediately challenged my usual spending habits. Impulsive by nature, I frequently spent money in an unguarded and spontaneous fashion. John, good friend that he was, knew that people like me shell out lots of money in the excitement of the moment for guitars, rowing machines, and good books, which despite terrific intentions, frequently get stored in the attic or in the back of the closet for lack of use. His suggestion was wise: spend $150 now on a good used bike, see if I were really serious about the sport, and spend more later if there was a need to do so and I was ready to commit myself to cycling several thousand miles a year. In the final analysis, I am glad I listened to John's advice because it ended up saving me a wad of cash.

That is the power of community in financial decision-making. That small piece of advice about recreational equipment can be profitably applied across the board to a number of decisions and expenditures. Friends who have a real Christian commitment and a loving concern for our financial well-being can help us sort through a wide variety of issues. We need brothers and sisters with whom we can share our budgets and work through issues like:

What are the most expedient and disciplined ways to get out of our current debt and stay out? Debt is no friend of Christian living. One expert suggests that this one factor keeps more people out of Christian service, Christian living, and Christian giving than any other single aspect of life. Certainly, it is difficult to say we have given "all to Jesus" when a significant portion of our financial future is tied up in credit cards and bank loans. It is the wise course for individuals and families, as quickly as possible, to alleviate the debt that holds a death grip on their witness for Christ.

How much money is appropriate to spend on such budgetary items as entertainment, cars, vacations, and insurance in a world that has a huge proportion of people dying because of economic lack? Ron Sider pointedly challenges us: "How will we respond to the desperate plight of the world's poor? Ten thousand persons died today because of inadequate food. One billion people are mentally retarded or physically deformed because of a poor diet. . . . North Americans live on an affluent island amid a sea of starving humanity. . . . We all know how subtle the materialistic temptations are and how convincing the rationalizations. Only by God's grace and with great effort can we escape the shower of luxuries which has almost suffocated our Christian compassion. All of us face this problem."[14]

How can my family increase the percentage of our income appropriated for financial offerings to kingdom causes? Many churches espouse the tithe—or 10 percent of a family's income—to be designated to the church. I agree with Richard Foster, however, who after examining both the Old and New Testament data suggests that

The tithe is not a sufficiently radical concept. . . . The tithe is not necessarily evil; it simply cannot provide a sufficient base for Jesus' call to carefree unconcern over provision. It fails to dethrone the rival god of materialism. It can never bring the freedom and liberality which is to characterize economic fellowship among the children of the kingdom. Perhaps the tithe can be a beginning way to acknowledge God as the owner of all things, but it is only a beginning and not an ending.[15]

Several books on Christian finances suggest percentages of income to be allocated for each budgetary category. For instance, for Family A, a family of four with an income of $20,000, the guidelines might recommend:

10% on giving ($2,000)
26% on housing ($5,200)
15% on food ($3,000)

The same guide would suggest that another family of four, Family B, who happens to make $60,000, should spend:

10% on giving ($6,000)
18% on housing ($10,800)
7% on food ($4,200)

Do you detect the fallacy in thinking here? Just because Family B makes more money, they are advised to spend (in real dollars) nearly twice as much on housing and $1,200 more on food while their percentage of giving remains the same. Do needs change just because someone earns more? Spending more because you make more might be the norm in our capitalistic society, but it is not necessarily the best choice for Christians trying to maximize their finances for God. As our "earning power" increases, our giving power should take a proportional leap as well. From 10 percent to 12 percent to 50 percent and higher. Our desire should be to hold down most expenses while seeking to increase giving as much as possible. In a few moments we will examine one of history's shining examples of this kind of thinking.

How can we consistently teach our children sound financial principles? Materialism, debt, and greed contribute to unhappiness, rampant divorce, and unsound Christian living at every turn. That is why the Lord instructs us to teach our children diligently the precepts of our faith. If we wait for the world or merely the anvil of personal experience to shape our children, we and they will be sorely disappointed. Educational voids are always filled—for good and frequently ill—and instruction in financial matters tends to be one of the voids.

How much should we save for such items as emergencies, future college tuition, and retirement? If you desire to send your kids on to college—or even help them out—you had better know that college expenses are currently outrunning inflation. It is predicted that in the year 2007 (the year my son Caleb would likely go to college if he so chooses) a private school will cost $40,000 a year. If true, that economic reality requires a mixture of faith and planning. And there are other similar economic realities that deserve prayerful consideration.

Does this particular major purchase (bike? boat? grill? easy chair?) or investment (mutual fund? bonds? ministry?) reflect responsible Christian giving and living? "Responsible" might be defined in many ways, but terms like frugal, safe, profitable, delayed gratification, and Christlike come immediately to my mind. To be carefree and childlike with our funds does not mean to foolishly throw them to the wind. The input of individuals with the mind of Christ can help us immensely.

Is my lifestyle simple, frugal, and joyfully free from the crush of materialism? I have profited from tips by several creative thinkers who propose a more simple lifestyle, including:

- learning to laugh at Madison Avenue advertisements (TV, magazine, radio) that are manipulative and blatantly dishonest.
- rejecting the flow of fashions (especially clothes and cars).
- sharing with friends such items as mowers, sports equipment, cars, and books.
- enjoying what you can get for free, check out, or borrow.
- learning to buy used goods of all kinds.
- accessing low-cost alternatives such as garage sales and thrift shops.
- gardening.

The possibilities are limited only by our creativity and commitment. But the joy increases as you find ways to enjoy a simple and frugal approach to life and reject the maddening squeeze of our culture's attitudes toward money and materialism.

It is likely, however, that if we do not allow others to sensitively challenge us, the questions that most need to be posed may not be asked at all. The flip side is this: if we do ask these questions of ourselves and with others seek solutions in light of God's work in this world, we will likely find a kind of liberation and joyous freedom that is very rare indeed. Such inquiries must not become legalistic in nature lest they become deadening. Rather, they should be guides to inspire us to a more Christlike model of living as His responsible and joyful servants.

John Wesley: A Shining Financial Example

John Wesley was one of England's most wealthy citizens — sort of. The qualification is apropos because actually, while Wesley had one of the highest earned incomes in his nation, he refused to accumulate wealth. His story is a living example of the impact of a budget and a life of giving in a world of need.

Early in his career and before his conversion, Wesley was elected a fellow of Lincoln College, Oxford University, where he was paid a healthy wage of thirty pounds a year. The position afforded him a comfortable living and some discretionary funds which he promptly expended on such amenities as playing cards, tobacco, and brandy. While employed in such comparatively innocent activity, Wesley one day encountered a chambermaid. She was ill-clad for a blustery English winter and the soft-hearted Oxford don decided to give her some money to amend the situation. He reached into his pocket for a bit of charity but found little; he had just finished paying for a few pictures for his room and was virtually broke.

The thought struck him with force: the Lord must certainly be displeased!

Will the Master say, "Well done, good and faithful steward"? Thou hast adorned thy walls with the money which might have screened this poor creature from the cold! O justice! O mercy! Are not these pictures the blood of this poor maid?[16]

Wesley's convictions on such matters motivated him to lay down a budget for himself. He decided that he needed twenty-eight pounds a year to live comfortably and responsibly, and he determined to give the rest away to the poor. In his first year on such a budget, he was able to give two pounds to the needy. The next year, however, his income almost doubled. With his budget as his guide, he again lived on twenty-eight pounds and gave away over half his entire income. The increase in giving and the maintenance of a similar level of expenses continued.[17]

WESLEY'S BUDGET

	Income	Living expenses	To the poor
First year	30 pounds	28 pounds (93%)	2 pounds (7%)
Second year	60 pounds	28 pounds (47%)	32 pounds (53%)
Third year	90 pounds	28 pounds (31%)	62 pounds (69%)
Fourth year	120 pounds	28 pounds (23%)	92 pounds (77%)
Eventually	over 1,400 pounds	30 pounds (2%)	over 1,400 pounds (98%)

In evaluating this powerful example for contemporary application, the points should be made that inflation was nil in his day so that expenses could be kept constant and that he had no dependents for which he needed to take financial responsibility.

Nonetheless, Wesley's principle of keeping expenses down while increasing giving was, and is, a sound pattern for maximizing God's financial gifts to Christians and a powerful reminder of what can be done through careful budgeting and frugal living.

Of course, Wesley's example lent power to his words. In his sermon "The Use of Money" he suggested a few questions people should "calmly and seriously" ask before purchasing something for themselves or their families.

● Am I acting herein, not as a proprietor, but as a steward of my Lord's goods?

- Am I doing this in obedience to His Word? In what Scripture does He require me so to do?
- Can I offer up this action, this expense, as a sacrifice to God through Jesus Christ?
- Have I reason to believe, that for this very work I shall have a reward at the resurrection of the just?

Wesley thought that an earnest and honest appraisal of these four questions would furnish his readers and listeners "clear light as to the way wherein you should go."[18] Just in case doubt remained concerning a purchase, however, Wesley suggested a pointed prayer.

> Try whether you can say to the Searcher of hearts, your conscience not condemning you,
> "Lord, Thou seest I am going to expend this sum, on that food, apparel, furniture. And Thou knowest, I act therein with a single eye, as a steward of Thy goods, expending this portion of them thus, in pursuance of the design Thou hadst in entrusting me with them. Thou knowest I do this in obedience to Thy Word, as Thou commandest, and because Thou commandest it. Let this, I beseech Thee, be a holy sacrifice, acceptable through Jesus Christ! And give me a witness in myself, that for this labour of love, I shall have a recompense, when Thou rewardest every man according to his works."
> Now if your conscience bear you witness in the Holy Ghost, that this prayer is well pleasing to God, then have you no reason to doubt, but that expense is right and good, and such as will never make you ashamed.[19]

What would happen if small groups—families, pastoral teams, discipleship groups—began prayerfully placing such questions and confessions at the forefront of their venture? Wouldn't it be wonderful to experience a spiritual revolution in the way we approach our finances and the way we invest our money and lives for the kingdom!

If guidelines were one facet of Wesleyan discipleship, prophetic utterance was another. Here are, for instance, some excerpts from Wesley's sermon discussing the verse "Lay not up for yourselves treasures upon earth" (Matt. 6:19, KJV).

For high eating and drinking, fine clothes and fine houses, state and equipage, gay pleasures and diversions, do all of them naturally hurt and disorder our heart. They are the food and nourishment of all the folly and weakness of our nature. . . . They are contrary to that sobriety and piety of heart, which relishes divine things.

Every man ought to provide the plain necessaries of life, both for his own wife and children. . . . not delicacies; not superfluities . . . whosoever, I say, being already in these circumstances, seeks a still larger portion on earth; he lives in an open, habitual denial of the Lord that bought him. "He hath" practically "denied the faith, and is worse than" an . . . "infidel."

When will ye be persuaded to choose the better part; that which cannot be taken away from you? . . . You have murdered your own soul! You have extinguished the last spark of spiritual life therein! Now indeed, in the midst of life, you are in death! You are a living man, but a dead Christian! Your affections are set, not on things above, but on things of the earth; on poor husks, that may poison, but cannot satisfy an everlasting spirit made for God. . . . You have thrown away the treasure in heaven. God and Christ are lost! You have gained riches — and hell-fire!

Wesley's aim was that his converts seek after "the plain necessaries," which he defined as simple "food to eat, raiment to put on, whatever nature moderately requires for preserving the body in health and strength." All else should be invested in the Lord's work and the needs of the world.

As already intimated, Wesley was willing to live up to what surely seem to us lofty notions. He ate and dressed very modestly and wrote that "if I leave behind me 10 pounds . . . you and all mankind bear witness against me that I lived and died a thief and a robber." Upon his death no one was disappointed. But a few along the way wondered how such integrity could exist. The Commissioners of Excise, for instance,

thought Wesley a bit negligent in reporting his entire hold-
ings of valuables. After examining his return they wrote a
letter expecting him to confess. Surely with such income he
was either careless or not telling the truth. "[We] cannot
doubt but you have [silver] plate for which you have hitherto
neglected to make an entry." Wesley fired back a response in
September 1776: "I have two silver spoons at London and
two at Bristol. This is all the plate I have at present, and I
shall not buy any more while so many round me want
bread."[19]

Can this kind of living take place today? Does the example
of Wesley provide a viable alternative in this day and age?
Surely, we must contend, the principles are built on solid
rock: simple living and eating, budgeting by holding expenses
to a minimum while increasing giving, asking bold questions
of ourselves and each other—all these are wise courses toward Christian discipleship and accountability in any age and
a way to begin getting a grip on important financial considerations.

The Community of Financial Accountability
One church that I know has a membership covenant challenging every member to a number of disciplines including involvement in a missions group, daily prayer and Bible study,
weekly worship, and proportional giving of finances which
begins with a tithe of gross income. In my mind, that is a
good start toward holistic Christianity. It is impressive to me
that in an attempt at authentically working out their corporate faith, responsible use of and accountability for personal
finances is a primary goal. It should be ours as well.

This issue of money can be a touchy one, however. We
must be careful not to force people into an area of discipleship for which they are not ready. Speaking on accountability
in a church one evening, I was challenged by someone who
asked, "Do you have any idea how many lives have been
wrecked and turned off from the Lord because of these 'hard
questions' you keep talking about?" His body language and
tone of voice alerted me to keep silent and listen. Raised in a
local church that had used manipulation in many areas of the
spiritual life, he needed to air out his feelings.

But I had an answer to his question. Yes, I think I have an idea how many people have been turned off by "hard questions"—from the pulpit, from harsh conversations, from insensitive teaching. I can only guess how many people won't even come to church anymore because they have grown weary of the "tithe sermon" and the pastor's continual fund appeals. But there is a flip side too. I know plenty of people whose lives have been laid waste because they would not let anybody hold them accountable for their lives, their dreams, their actions, and yes—even their budgets. I know of all kinds of good folk who have allowed money to creep in and choke their entire worldview. I know of Christians who—with no accountability—are sinking into massive debt from which it will take years to recover. Unlike the liberation Burkett promises, they suffer captivity.

The church of Jesus Christ must find ways to make responsible and liberating accountability in the area of finances an attractive reality for her people. The sharing, and sharpening, of practical personal finances must be made available to everyone who is wise enough to take heed. If the God of both Testaments thought it important enough to forcefully emphasize this subject, we must not argue.

A BUDGET WORKSHEET (monthly)

Categories

Total Monthly Gross Income _____

Giving (*Church and other offerings*)	_____
Savings	
Retirement	_____
Children's college	_____
Other	_____
Total	_____
Taxes/Social security	_____
Debt reduction	_____
Housing	_____
Home repairs	
Food	_____
Transportation	_____
Utilities	_____
Phone	_____
Insurance	
Disability	_____
Life	_____
Auto	_____
Other	_____
Total	_____
Clothing	_____
Medical	_____
Entertainment	_____
Vacations	_____
Gifts	_____
Subscriptions	_____
Child toys/diapers/etc.	_____
Books	_____
Miscellaneous	_____

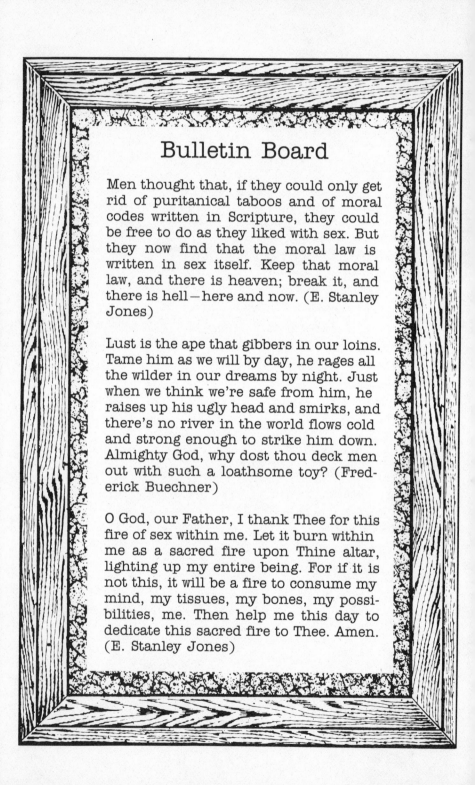

Bulletin Board

Men thought that, if they could only get rid of puritanical taboos and of moral codes written in Scripture, they could be free to do as they liked with sex. But they now find that the moral law is written in sex itself. Keep that moral law, and there is heaven; break it, and there is hell—here and now. (E. Stanley Jones)

Lust is the ape that gibbers in our loins. Tame him as we will by day, he rages all the wilder in our dreams by night. Just when we think we're safe from him, he raises up his ugly head and smirks, and there's no river in the world flows cold and strong enough to strike him down. Almighty God, why dost thou deck men out with such a loathsome toy? (Frederick Buechner)

O God, our Father, I thank Thee for this fire of sex within me. Let it burn within me as a sacred fire upon Thine altar, lighting up my entire being. For if it is not this, it will be a fire to consume my mind, my tissues, my bones, my possibilities, me. Then help me this day to dedicate this sacred fire to Thee. Amen. (E. Stanley Jones)

CHAPTER FIVE

Sex

Pastor Ben Haden recently encountered an unusual couple from West Virginia. "We've been dating for over a year," they said. "We're both Christians. We sleep on every date, but we always end up with a prayer."
"How's that?" said Haden.
"We sleep on every date" — meaning sex on every date — "but we always end up with a prayer."
"What do you pray for?"
"We pray a prayer of repentance," they replied.
A very bad theology of sex. A very bad theology of repentance. A very bad theology, period.
There is confusion among Christians concerning sex. How do we handle it? If God made us this way, why can't we just enjoy it?
The rampant sexual indulgence of our culture has led us to incredible difficulties. And the problems are legion: lust; adultery; abuse; pre- and extramarital sex; homo-, bi-, and transsexuality; rape; molestation; pornography. Stanley Jones, fifty years ago, wrote words that resonate today perhaps more than ever:

They tell us that the word "Bedlam" used to be [the word] "Bethlehem" — the place of the birth of Christ has changed to the name of a place of confusion. Is this not what has happened sexually in our day? Bethlehem, symbol of the birth of a Child — the epitome of sex in its most beautiful and tender phase — now degenerates into a veritable "Bedlam" of sex frustration and defeat. Why? . . .
No age ever emphasized sex more than this age has

done, or enjoyed sex less. Restraints are gone; Puritanism has been banished. But now that the age is free to do as it likes, it finds it doesn't like what it does.[1]

James Dobson cites anthropologist J.D. Unwin who, after studying eighty-eight civilizations throughout world history, reported some startling conclusions. Each culture, he said, reflected a similar life cycle beginning with a strict code of sexual conduct and ending with a demand for "freedom" — the throwing off of traditional constraints in order to express individual passion. Unwin suggests that *every* society which allowed such sexual permissiveness soon perished.

The Bible, as does responsible contemporary research, calls us to upright sexual relations. But the Christian need not run from sex just because there is potential for danger. God intended something special when He created sexual beings. His people picked up on this idea early in revelational history, and therefore the Hebrews did not treat the human body and its functions as evil, shameful, or indecent.[2] Rather, they celebrated life and sexuality, as can be seen in many ways, not the least being what many people consider an unusual inclusion in the biblical canon — the Song of Songs. This book unashamedly celebrates sexuality, human love, and tenderness. It is God's call to fulfill our potential as sexual creatures whom He declared "good." The call of this and other scriptural admonitions is to celebrate God's gift of sexuality within the parameters He has established.

This chapter is not designed to explore all the avenues to sexual wholeness as individuals and as the people of God. But perhaps it can help. With the current confusion and disarray concerning sexuality, even within our Christian ranks (some would say *especially!*), there should be saints bold enough to ask their brothers and sisters some redemptive questions in order to support and hold each other accountable for healthy, wholesome, holy sexuality. Our cultures, both Christian and national, depend on our response to the challenge.

Time for Some Hard Questions
In the summer of 1987, I was invited to teach in a theological graduate school in Nairobi, Kenya. While there, I was bom-

barded with questions about evangelical America and all our seeming lapses. The concern and interest of these African friends were piqued by the well-publicized sexual scandals plaguing America's Christian and political worlds at that time. Jim Bakker, Jimmy Swaggart, and presidential candidate Gary Hart, to name some of the higher profile media stars, were engaging in some fancy footwork and damage control to preserve their careers. Some of the scandals were easily understood and explained. And I assured my international students that many positive things were happening in my homeland regardless of those who had had their flings with infidelity.

But my wife, staying in Texas during my seven-week stint overseas, clipped an article from the *Dallas Morning News* that really put a damper on my spirit. Opening the fragile airmail envelope, I was greeted by a snippet of newsprint that left me stunned. One of the evangelical leaders I truly admired had fallen. Gordon MacDonald, president of Inter-Varsity Christian Fellowship, best-selling author, and sought-after speaker, had admitted to an adulterous relationship in late 1984 and early 1985. He had since confessed and repented of the indiscretion and was maintaining a strong marriage with his wife of twenty-five years. But rumors had begun circulating and he felt obliged to resign his influential position.

I was floored. The downfalls of some people had not been surprising. But this man whose ministry I knew and admired? Whose books I read and quoted? Someone to whom I could point as a man of integrity with a rock-solid marriage and a book that explained righteous relationships? Someone I felt certain was above reproach?

About a month later, MacDonald was interviewed in *Christianity Today*. He described, briefly, how the affair had come about, asked forgiveness, and then reported why he felt the need to confess publicly and resign his presidency. *CT* quotes MacDonald in this revealing passage:

> Satan's ability to distort the heart and the mind is beyond belief. I assume the responsibility for what I did; I made those decisions out of a distorted heart.
>
> In addition, I now realize I was lacking in mutual ac-

countability through personal relationships. We need friendships where one man regularly looks another man in the eye and asks questions about our moral life, our lust, our ambitions, our ego.[3]

The interview was refreshing because MacDonald admitted both his failure and his need for accountability, and noted that he and his wife had begun to cultivate friendships on a much deeper level than in the past. In addition, he began to relate to three trusted Christian leaders who had "pronounced him guilty of adultery, acknowledged his repentance, advised him to cut back on his speaking engagements, and required that he account to them spiritually on a regular basis."[4]

Evangelical America can rejoice in the results. MacDonald is back in the saddle again, ministering, speaking, writing, and helping others in the process of healing. Hopefully, those of us eager to fulfill our kingdom potential will not wait for such tragedy before we cultivate accountable relationships and examine our sexuality. We need to engage in both now. Said one Michigan pastor currently in an accountability group, "Many Christians and most ministers think they are above the problems related to sex. They're not. We all need help."

What Makes for Good Sex

There are plenty of good books on Christians and sex. There are even a few excellent ones on how to engage in successful intercourse from the time the couple enters the honeymoon suite till "death do us part." I concede those areas of inquiry for now. Allow me to sidestep the marriage bed and sexual technique in this chapter and talk about the other things that will benefit your sexual relationship.

Be a zealous monogamist

The sexual revolutionists of the past three decades tried to hook us on the abysmal idea that sex outside of marriage enhances a loving relationship. These "experts" based their contentions on folklore, not on good research, and certainly not on the Bible. Scripture throws up red flags at such ideas, and the consequences of ignoring the warnings are borne out by the moral universe. Blumstein and Schwartz, in *American*

Couples, found that "husbands and wives who had had extra-marital sex were more likely to break up, whether it happened at the beginning of the marriage or after many years. . . . For most heterosexuals, non-monogamy is associated with less commitment to a future together."[5] The researchers found that cohabitation before marriage wasn't a good send-off to loving relationship either. "Cohabitors" were found to be two to four times more likely than married couples to dissolve their relationships. Chances for affairs were twice as great. Says Tim Stafford, "A partner's infidelity is more than just a disappointing choice . . . but a stab in the gut. It threatens any relationship, regardless of how loving."[6]

Partners in a marriage need to settle in and recognize that the greatest of God's blessings comes when two partners abstain sexually until their wedding night, and stay loyal to a monogamous relationship infused by the Holy Spirit till "death do us part." Stafford is blunt and right on target. "Marriage demands, positively, that we make a pledge to love for life. Negatively, it demands that we abhor adultery. To brush aside that rule, emphasizing the positive pledge without the negative command, is to kid yourself. Adultery destroys the possibilities of Eden."[7]

We shouldn't be surprised when Paul Pearsall, a sex therapist from the Kinsey Institute, affirms what ought to be obvious in light of the biblical ethic.

> Super marital sex is the most erotic, intense, fulfilling experience any human being can have. Anonymous sex with multiple partners pales by comparison. . . . No form of extramarital sex can compete with super marital sex, and once this lesson is learned, spouses having affairs may begin cheating on their "lovers," and having "intramarital" sex with their husband or wife.[8]

Blessed are the zealous monogamists . . .

> those who remain attuned to the entire biblical teaching concerning family, interpersonal relationships, selfless love and service, and yes, even sex,
> for they will find wholeness.

Remember the loving touch

The poll stands out in the memories of many. It was instigated by advice columnist Ann Landers who, in response to a dare from one of her readers, asked her female audience to take a moment and respond to the question: Would you be content to be held close and treated tenderly and forget about "the act"? Upward of 90,000 women responded. The results are memorable, as were the mountains of mail that swamped Landers' office. A whopping 72 percent said yes. Genital contact was not the turn-on for these women. Loving care, tenderness, closeness—these things were the stuff of a loving relationship. Typical of the responses was this line from Texarkana.

> Without the tender embrace the act is animalistic. For years I hated sex and felt used. I was relieved when my husband died. My present mate is on heart pills that have made him impotent. It's like heaven to be held and cuddled.[9]

As a general rule, men and women are wired differently. We men are charged by the short romp in the bed we see portrayed by Hollywood. Women are attuned to the caress, the unselfish forethought, and tender talk both before, during, and after sex. In fact, as James Dobson suggests, "Because women are more romantically inclined, the man who wants an exciting sexual relationship with his wife should focus on the *other* 23½ hours in the day. He should compliment her, bring her flowers and tell her that he cares. These are the ingredients of genuine passion."[10]

Be a friend

Not everyone would consider a marriage mate as best friend. We should. And we should take the time and energy to make that label a reality. Friends want to be together and will search for regular and creative ways to do so. Couples too should plan activities and engage in recreation together. Enjoyable time spent together will foster the sort of intimate friendship that God intended for husband and wife.

Friends engage in meaningful conversation. Sadly, many

married couples communicate less with time. This could not
be because we know each other better, for the nature of
conversation is such that the more intimate friends are, the
richer communication becomes. No, we talk less because we
become lazy. I have noticed this tendency in my relationship
to my wife Mary. As the years roll by in our marriage, I have
been prone to sink into a silent slouch in my easy chair. On
the other hand, some of our best communication takes place
when our son is tucked soundly in bed and we just "hang
out" in the living room and talk about us, the future, the
events of the day, our problems. These "friendly" chats make
the stuff necessary for friendship and renewal within marriage.

Some of us wonder what in the world we should talk about
if we decide to repent of our silence and engage in some real
conversation. While not intended as an absolute panacea, this
short list of discussion starters by Alice Fryling[11] (with slight
revision) challenges couples to get the talk flowing. Next
time you wonder what to talk about, let these questions get
you started. Think you know all about your spouse? I doubt
it!

What are five things I do that say to you "I love you"?

What do you wish I did (that I don't do often) to say "I
love you"?

What activity that we did together last week did you
enjoy most? Last month? Last year?

What are two things you hope will happen in our relationship in the next year?

What do you like to talk about the most? People—who?
Things—what? Places—where? Ideas—what?

Describe the most frightening moment you have ever
endured. The happiest. The saddest. The most em-
barrassing.

What's the best book you ever read? Best movie you ever saw? Best song you ever heard?

What things have we done together that have been the most fun?

What are your most cherished memories from ages 1–10? 10–20? 20–30? After that?

What did you want to be "when you grew up"? At 5? 15? 20? 25? Now?

How would you like for me to pray for you this week?

What does forgiveness mean to you? In what ways have you forgiven me this week?

What are some things I do to make you laugh or feel good?

How do you hear God speaking to you?

If someone gave you $1,000, or a week's vacation, or the chance to meet anybody in contemporary society or history, what would you do with that gift?

What is something you really like about my father? My mother? Your father? Your mother?

Who was the best teacher you ever had? What did you learn from that person?

What was your greatest success ever? Failure?

What do you like best about our children?

What is one dream that you have had about life that hasn't been fulfilled yet? An unfulfilled dream about our marriage? Our family?

Is our physical relationship what you hoped it would be? Why? Why not?

What is the best gift anyone ever gave you? What gift have I given you that you liked the most?

List ten adjectives that describe you best. How about ten for me?

What is the most important thing you do on an average day? The most important thing I do?

What is the hardest feeling for you to express? How can I help you express it?

What is something that you enjoy about your days, but don't talk about much?

When did you first know you loved me?

If you are like me, you probably wanted to start penciling your own questions in the margin. Go ahead. But remember to eventually pick that pencil up from the page and start asking. You will laugh some. Cry some. Be driven to query further. Whatever the outcome, this kind of give-and-take develops friendship and meaning within marriage. Leave your judge's robe in the closet. Develop your listening skills. And remember, rich communication lays the foundation for a truly loving, sexual relationship. Talk on!

Use marriage resources
Excellent videos, books, personality inventories, marriage enrichment seminars, and other helpful aids abound. But they are fruitless unless husband-and-wife teams use them. Check your local Christian bookstore for a variety of materials that will undoubtedly broaden your perspective and enrich your life together. And, to add some fun to the approach, invite some friends. Since our church library stocks a number of excellent videos on marriage and the family, one of my friends at the seminary asked me to check some out for her

small group. She and her friends planned to park themselves in a VCR-endowed living room and enjoy the videos together—a good idea on her part. Opportunities abound which each of us can take advantage of. We should discipline ourselves now to begin pursuing some of these avenues of education.

Singleness

Some singles feel that God has given them the gift of celibacy and that their calling is to use that gift to more fully concentrate their time and energies on the Lord's work. I consider such a gift a blessing which can be used to great effect for the kingdom of God. Paul was, as far as we can tell, single. Jesus was single. Nearly all the church fathers were single. These men as well as other men and women who constitute a sizable portion of the "giants" of Christian history could not have accomplished what they were called to do if they had been married. They were free from certain time constraints, monetary concerns, and persistent family matters. If celibacy and singleness is your calling, you have the support and blessing of Christian history and of Scripture. And, lest we forget, Paul forcefully stated his pronouncement on this issue in his initial letter to the Corinthians when he said to the unmarried and widows, "It is good . . . to stay unmarried, as I am" (1 Cor. 7:8).

But some singles want to be married. Many worry about how to harness and subdue their sexual energy. Some feel like they are "all dressed up with no place to go." The large majority of singles sense no call to the celibate lifestyle. Christians should take note. Singleness is a mode of life that we should not take lightly. The single population is growing and represents one of the major demographic trends of recent decades.

I wish there were easy answers for singles who desire to have their sexuality fulfilled within marriage but for one reason or another have not yet found that relationship. I agree with Tim Stafford who urges church singles groups to begin helping people see celibacy as a gift—a positive witness to the world for either a short period or an entire lifetime. Stafford reminds us that Paul told the saints in Corinth if they found themselves slaves, and recognized they could not gain freedom, they then should live as good slaves. Further, if you are married then you should live faithfully, even to a pagan spouse (1 Cor. 7:12-14). Extrapolated to the single state, perhaps it could be said that if you find yourself single, and not wanting to be, be the single person God would want you to be — upholding His standards, seeing your current celibacy as a genuine gift and opportunity for witness, living fully in ways impossible to the heavily entrenched spouse and parent.

The support of a group helps. A group that lifts, queries, prays, and practically moves to aid the frailties of its members will be greatly useful in maintaining purity in an impure world. I speak from experience. In my single days it was an accountability group peppering me with questions and holding me up in loving care that laid the good foundation my wife and I now share. I am a debtor to those guys.

Other Problems
Because of the wreckage that the sexual revolution has dealt the Christian world, the problems many of us face are, as already stated, legion. Molestation, rape, hyper-adultery; abuse; homo-, bi-, and transsexuality; and so forth plague us and have led to excessive proportions of compulsive disorders that require special attention. In the area of sexuality, we need loving support groups more than ever. Donald Joy offers this comment:

> I used to talk about reparenting such people. Now I am delighted with the new findings about healing for compulsive disorders. These include the sexual addict. We commonly find this deep damage associated with catalytic environments such as child abuse, alcoholism in a parent, and authoritarianism in the family of origin. . . .
> Healing for the promiscuous requires something deeper than dealing with sexual problems. And that healing requires a special grace administered in a healing community. Typically a confidential support group of three to six people, to whom the entire history of failure is disclosed, is just the right environment in which complete healing can take place. But the time frame re-

quires from one to three years of high investment. The group provides the healing, forgiving, and reconstructing foundation. The grace of Jesus is the agent for the change, but people must do again for the person what parents do for young children: provide tangible feedback that fills the tank of self-respect, based on significant, unconditionally affirming relationships.[12]

Joy contends that a loosely structured group, dedicated to health and wholeness and willing to plumb the depths of the deepest subjects—including sex—can add to each of our lives, regardless of how heavily entrenched the problems seem to be.

If Ever There Were a Need for Accountability . . .
Occasionally someone will approach me and say something like this: "That's just not my problem. I simply don't struggle with sexual sin." Whenever somebody says that, I watch carefully over the next one or two years. Once such a claim is made, the devil often attacks. The very same individual who suggested that he was not vulnerable to such temptations may soon be floundering in an abyss of sexual immorality. We all should begin, as one author suggests, creating "hedges" to guard us from possible falls. Bill Hybels, pastor and author, picks up on this theme.

> If we do not set up guidelines to establish accountability, we are inviting trouble. Recently, a pastor of a major church was exposed in having multiple adulterous relationships. When I asked him how this could have happened, he replied that he had created an environment where he had to answer to no one.[13]

In this area, particularly, we need to be answerable to somebody. Our culture is working hard against the Christian norm on this one. The media pours its crooked perspective into our minds daily. Broken families leave many of us without a living and breathing example of healthy relationships. Cultural expectations have sunk. As E. Stanley Jones intimated at the beginning of the chapter, we are dealing with bedlam indeed! Hybels is right: The evil one works hard to destroy God's design.

> He knows that a vibrant, mutually satisfying, and creative sex life will bind two people together with cords that cannot break. The bond will produce a healthy marriage and family for another generation. God will be glorified and the evil one will suffer defeat.[14]

Good sex. There is a price. And there is a satanic plot conspiring against Christians to make sure they don't pay it. We must join forces and combat the direction in which such diabolical assault would lead us.

Bulletin Board

Walk and be healthy. The best way to lengthen out our days is to walk steadily and with a purpose. (Charles Dickens)

The civilized man has built a coach, but he has lost the use of his feet. (Ralph Waldo Emerson)

Doctors should tell us what exercise does for people: the decrease of fatigue, the increase in energy, the measurable improvement in physical work capacity, the enhancement of self-image. (George Sheehan)

Physically fit people are more intellectually inclined, emotionally stable, composed, self-confident, easygoing and relaxed. The very act of keeping in shape reinforces these personality attributes. (A.H. Ismail, Purdue University)

di · et (di et) n. [‹ Gr. *diaita*, way of life]

It is fascinating to know that one can grow healthier as one grows older and not necessarily the reverse! (Paul Dudley White)

CHAPTER SIX

Health

Matt, I've got good news and bad news."
I said "Uh-huh" but what I thought was *Oh-oh!*
The University of Kansas was using some fancy technology to perform fitness tests on certain members of our track team. The researchers needed my participation as a discus thrower in order to get data on not only runners and jumpers, but large and relatively muscular throwers as well. Treadmill tests, blood tests, muscle biopsy tests to determine fast and slow twitch fibers, underwater weighing to investigate body-fat content, and other experiments assessed current health and provided data to predict future performance. At the end of the myriad procedures the professor called me in to discuss the results. Hence the "good news, bad news" pronouncement.

His voice sounded ominous, and I sucked in a breath of air to brace myself for his diagnosis. "The good news," the doctor said, "is you're still alive."

Swell. I could hardly wait for the second part of the outline.

"The bad news is, *you're not going to be for very long if you don't start eating and exercising right!*"

"Imagine that!" I thought to myself. More than just a little piqued, I defensively began reviewing my current status. I had been on a top-notch track and field team for four years now, had won the Big Eight Championship in my event, had recently been invited to try out for the U.S. Olympic team, would soon be named All-American in my event, worked out from two to eight hours a day—six days a week—and "Doc" was telling me I was out of shape and possibly in mortal danger! I didn't understand, but I was all ears. He was the Ph.D. and had both my respect and attention.

Spirituality Includes Physical Health!

As I began to put the plans together for this book, I was not certain I wanted to include a chapter on physical fitness. "Will people consider it too frivolous or worldly?" I wondered. The more I researched, however, the more I became convinced that this subject is rarely considered carefully enough by Christians interested in pursuing the disciplines of the spiritual life.

I now wish, unabashedly, that fitness experts could get the attention of Christians. If we would lend them our ears and a few hours out of our week, it could have substantial impact on our kingdom potential. Most Christians, I have found, are in no better physical shape—sometimes worse—than the secular world. And with the work of God before us, this is inexcusable. I am also beginning to think it is bad theology.

Throughout Christian history some have thought of spirituality exclusively in terms of the nonphysical, immortal part of people.[1] To live spiritually meant to detach oneself from the throes of this world and attempt to transcend to a higher, more exalted plane. This is quite foreign, of course, to the Hebrew mind-set and the backdrop of biblical revelation. In the Semitic understanding of humanity, which extends then to the New Testament, a person was not a soul with a body, or a body with a soul. Persons were understood as "body-souls." Scholar Marvin Wilson contributes the following:

> None of the Hebrew terms translated "soul" or "spirit" refers to the nonphysical part of a human being; this is dualistic Greek thinking, which, unfortunately, has influenced our understanding of these English terms. In Hebraic thought, "soul" or "spirit" refers to the whole person or individual as a living being. It stands for the person himself. . . . In short, human beings live as souls; they do not "have" souls.[2]

Interesting then that Paul, undoubtedly aware of the Greek perspective, did not conceive of the salvation of the soul apart from the body; salvation meant the redemption of the body as well (Rom. 8:21-23). I don't want to stretch the Book of Romans to suggest that God was trying to specifically tell us to sign up for the next aerobics class or begin jogging four miles a day as part of our salvation. But it is interesting that: *Paul alludes to the body and exercise in his writings.*

- Do not offer the parts of your body to sin, as instruments of wickedness, but . . . to Him as instruments of righteousness! (Rom. 6:13)
- Your body is a temple of the Holy Spirit. . . . Therefore, honor God with your body (1 Cor. 6:19).
- Therefore, I urge you, brothers, in view of God's mercy, to offer your bodies as living sacrifices, holy and pleasing to God (Rom. 12:1).
- You don't need to be reminded that while many may compete in a racing event, only one wins first prize, so go all out for the top place. . . . I put my body through terrific workouts and thoroughly master it, because I don't want to preach to others and wind up a dismal failure myself (1 Cor. 9:24-27, *Cotton Patch Version*).[3]
- I run the race then with determination. I am no shadow-boxer, I really fight! I am my body's sternest master, for fear that when I have preached to others I should myself be disqualified (vv. 26-27, PH).

Paul may well have utilized vigorous exercise in his own ministry. John Pollock's biography of Paul describes the apostle as he lived and waited in Tarsus before the bulk of his ministry began: "He enjoyed watching their [the Gentiles'] games. Too old to compete in athletics he probably joined in the calisthenics down by the river, stripping naked in the normal way, possibly boxing to harden his body for the tasks he was sure lay ahead."[4] Certainly he must have been hardy to survive the many physical trials he encountered.

The culture of the first century, at the level of exercise at least, was probably healthier than ours. There were significant cultural differences between modern-day America and agrarian Palestine. Fewer cars (!) and no public transport, to name a few.

If you wanted to get across town, or into the hills to pray, or to the next community twenty miles away—you walked. Plain and simple. Thus from biblical data and logical inference, we can assume that Jesus and His disciples put in plenty of miles most days as they ministered and worked for the kingdom. It was natural!

Beyond this specific physical activity, the practice of the whole culture — and hence most Christians of the day — was to vigorously work with your hands and feet for the large portion of the day. Whether your occupation was housewife or carpenter or farmer, walking, running, sweating, and breathing hard were normal. It was the kind of activity that contributed to health.

That's an extremely quick glance at some New Testament data. God took fitness seriously in the Old Testament too. Again, the culture was agrarian and full of walking and hard work. But beyond that, I find it fascinating that this Israelite God was a God of health. His people knew it; one of their Hebrew names for Him was *Jehovah-rapha* ("The Lord who heals"). It is wholly consistent then that this Deity sets up very specific prescriptions for health. For instance, He was concerned about:

- laws for sanitary disposal of excrement (Deut. 23:12-14),
- laws for cleanliness: diet, childbirth, infections (Lev. 11–15),
- laws for isolation and quarantine in case of contagious disease (Num. 5:1-4),
- and, laws for rest and leisure (Ex. 20:8-11; Lev. 25).

Further, the Israelites recognized that salvation was more than "a soul saved." Says Chaplain Robert B. Reeves, Jr.:

The biblical words for healing and salvation have the same root meaning in both the Hebrew and the Greek. The meaning is ultimately TO BE MADE WHOLE. The distinction we have made between them . . . applying healing to the body and salvation to the soul, is utterly alien to the Bible. Man's health is his salvation, and his salvation is his health; for both are signs of his wholeness as a creature.[5]

Listen to God's words in Isaiah concerning an ideal society:

I will create Jerusalem to be a delight. . . . The sound of weeping and of crying will be heard in it no more. Never again will there be in it an infant that lives but a few

days, or an old man who does not live out his years; he
who dies at a hundred will be thought a mere youth; he
who fails to reach a hundred will be considered accursed
(Isa. 65:18-20).

But the bottom line is not this or that verse. It is simply
that God wants us to maximize our gifts and capabilities for
Him. That is possible only as we seek to develop and maintain the bodily resources with which He has honored us.
Contemporary research, fortunately, is finding more and better ways to do that.

Exercise

We have become true believers in the benefits of exercise,
according to a recent article in *U.S. News and World Report.*
But, as studies show, intellectual assent does not necessarily
translate into healthy habits. "Most citizens," the article ad-
mits, "confine their practice to nothing more strenuous than
pushing a shopping cart around a supermarket on Saturday
morning or shoveling down a pint of ice cream while doing
laps between the kitchen and TV set."[6] A recent nationwide
study shows that 80–90 percent of Americans still do not get
enough exercise.

While perhaps variously defined, most experts today recognize good exercise as the "aerobic" type. Aerobic refers to a
number of exercises that stimulate heart and lung activity for
a time period sufficiently long to produce beneficial changes
in the body. The main objectives of an aerobic exercise program are to develop efficient lungs, an energetic heart, and a
good vascular (blood vessel) system. Aerobic exercises include brisk walking, running/jogging, roller skating, dancing,
swimming, and cycling. The most popular of these in 1988,
according to a survey by American Sports Data, Inc. were:

Fitness walking	13.2 million people
Running/jogging	8.5 million people
Stationary cycling	7.9 million people
Lap swimming	5.9 million people
Low-impact aerobics	2.2 million people
Treadmill exercise	0.9 million people

Exercise, in order to contribute to health, should be performed twenty to thirty minutes at a time, three to four days a week. Also, you should perform the exercise while aiming for a heart rate that will provide a "training effect." Below, an equation is given to figure whether you are arriving at such an effect in your exercise.

Subtract your age from 220.

Then take that figure minus your resting pulse (your "before I get out of bed" pulse).

Take that number times 65 percent if you are beginning, up to 85 percent if you are more advanced in your training.

Then add back in your resting pulse.

If you are diligent in trying to achieve aerobic fitness and get several months of proper exercise under your belt, many experts claim that you may begin enjoying a wide variety of benefits.

- Higher levels of energy in daily activities.
- Improved intellectual capacity and increased productivity.
- Better levels of concentration and increased perseverance in all daily tasks.
- Relief of stress and the bolstering of enthusiasm and optimism.
- A slower aging process.
- A realistic way to—along with responsible eating—control your weight.
- Stronger bones.
- Psychological well-being, release of tension, help with relaxation and better sleep.
- Help with controlling depression and other emotional disturbances.
- Significant added protection from heart disease, improved blood circulation, and the ability of the lungs, heart, and other organs and muscles to work more effectively together.

- Fewer aches and pains, including lower-back pain.
- Enhancement of sexual pleasure.

By the way, numerous items from the above list support the contention that exercise can contribute significantly to spiritual well-being. For instance, look at the first five items in the preceding list and see if they won't lead you to believe that saints can pray better, serve with greater zest, envision God's plans more effectively, live daily with more strength, and serve the kingdom of God on earth longer with aerobic activity than without. It is not hard to understand how God would be pleased with a regular program of aerobic exercise.

My problem at the University of Kansas was that all my exercise was isotonic (contraction of muscles plus the movement of joints), none aerobic. In short, I performed basic calisthenics, weight lifting and, of course, throwing of the discus. It was lots of hard work, and I sure felt like I was sweating enough and had enough muscle mass to be in shape. But nothing that I was doing contributed to cardiovascular or respiratory health. Was I in shape? For throwing a discus around, perhaps. But overall fitness? I was a health problem. I will never forget the words of the doctor: "Change your exercise habits, Matt. Get doing some aerobic activity quick, or you'll have heart disease in your early adulthood!"

Even with that caution, it is still all right for an individual to lift weights and do calisthenics. Those things will frequently help an athlete perform better in various sports activities and decrease one's likelihood of injury. But as Cooper says, "Special muscle-building and flexibility exercises must be done in addition to or in combination with—and not in place of—one of the primary aerobic programs."[7] In fact, Mark Paulsen, strength coach from the University of New Mexico, highly recommends a fifteen-minute program of push-ups, chin-ups, and sit-ups three times a week for those without access to a weight room. "It will help," he says, "stabilize and strengthen your whole body" while enroute to aerobic fitness.

A recent study in the *Journal of the American Medical Association* disclosed that even in men and women of relatively old age—specifically 86–96 in the study—a simple leg workout (three sets of eight repetitions) on a weight machine three times a week tripled muscle strength, increased muscle size 9 percent, and improved knee flexibility. Dr. Maria Fiatarone, study leader, reported a remarkable response. A nationwide study is slated to determine to what extent body building could help keep older people out of nursing homes.

If you are not already exercising, begin a program today. A few pointers might help you get started and keep going.

Step one. Get a thorough medical exam from a doctor able to administer a "stress test."

Step two. Determine your target heart rate.

Step three. Choose a basic aerobic exercise that you enjoy and will be able to stick with.

Step four. Start your aerobics program with sensible "warm-up" and "cool-down" periods. Warm-ups should consist of three or four minutes of not so demanding exercises. Cool downs should be at least five minutes and consist of a slow amble after exercising.

Step five. Try to stick with the aerobic program for at least six weeks. Commit yourself to that short-term period and you will find that you are likely to establish a habit. Sixty to seventy percent of adults who start exercising drop out in the first month. Stick with it . . . you will be glad you did. Dr. James Rippe calls this perseverance "the No. 1 exercise challenge."[8]

Step six. Be patient. Don't expect too much too soon. You may be a little sore for a while. Occasionally a little bored. Fatigued at times. But be patient. Unless you are preparing for a big race in the next month or two, you have time. Congratulate yourself for finally making progress toward wholeness and health.

Step seven. Find a partner, or several, to join you and hold you accountable to keep exercising. Those who persevere in a fitness program and those who quit can frequently be divided into two groups: those who participated regularly with friends in their exercise and those who did not! Besides, it is almost always more fun with fellowship.

Diet
Diet is not one of my favorite words. I suppose there are two reasons for that. First, I have never found one that felt very

good. Second, I have never found one that worked over the long haul. Every pound that I have ever lost on somebody's newfangled idea for weight loss eventually came back with a powerful vengeance.

That is why, when we talk of diet, it should not be something we begin today with plans to quit when we arrive at our destination. If that is the attitude, chances are you will regain all your weight, and more! Worse, it will be harder for you to lose weight the next time you try. Just reward, some say, for totally confusing the metabolic ability of your body. Our bodies are rather intelligent. When they sense they are being starved, they adjust. You can starve yourself and lose weight, to be sure. But when you begin eating normally again, you will find that your body has adjusted, so that it actually operates on fewer calories than when you began your starvation program. Result? You gain back your weight. All of it. Usually more.

The doctor at my university pointed out to me that the problem was not poor dieting procedure, but unwise eating, period. Trying to add as much weight and strength as possible, my daily intake consisted of several servings of red meat, a gallon of milk, six to twelve eggs, and plenty of pasta, butter-drenched potatoes, vegetables, sweets, and other assorted morsels. "Heart disease in your early adulthood" indeed. The doctor did not have to be a Ph.D. to see my problem. I went to the training table and opened my mouth, not my mind. He may have been exactly right too when he said that I was likely killing myself.

The Aerobics Center in Dallas, Texas has formulated some wise principles for establishing a healthy balance in eating habits.

- Develop a normal pattern of 50-20-30 percentage caloric balance among the three main food types: daily consume 50 percent complex carbohydrates, 20 percent from protein, and 30 percent from fats. (See a basic nutrition book to be able to recognize the difference!)
- If you want to lose weight, eat 25 percent of your daily calories at breakfast; 50 percent at lunch; 25 percent at supper. The idea is to eat most of your calories before supper. To maintain weight go for a 25-30-45 approach.

- Do your aerobic exercise just before the evening meal if you can. It will suppress your appetite.
- Beware consuming too few calories. It is unhealthy for your body and usually will not allow you to maintain your hard earned weight reduction.
- Learn the formula to determine the daily caloric intake for maintaining your ideal weight. It is as follows: Take your ideal body weight (see next section), multiply that number by 12 up to 40 years of age, and by 10 after that.

If you feel like you need a few more calories for energy, you should try multiplying your ideal body weight by 13 or 15, depending on whether you are over or under 40. If you are engaged in a job of manual labor for up to eight hours a day, or exercising so much that you are burning over 500 calories a day, multiply your ideal weight by 20, regardless of age.

Weight
Writing, like preaching, is good for me. I write, for instance, and recognize that my life does not match up with my prophetic pen. So, before this chapter on fitness was written, let me assure you that I was in a season of my life where I did not exercise regularly. I do now. My diet was a bit awry. It is, as of this writing, much improved. Nonetheless, this topic of ideal-weight research really proved to be a major challenge.

I am able to deceive myself. Looking in the mirror my eyes still see the version of the man I was in college. My eyes lie. I am not that man physically. In fact, when I began to look at the issue objectively I discovered I was far more overweight than I had ever dreamed. Cooper suggests this formula for an objective view.

- Men, take your height in inches, multiply that figure by 4, and then subtract 128.
- Women, take your height in inches, multiply it by 3.5 and then subtract 108.[9]

Next, get on a pair of accurate scales and see how you compare. If you are like me, and many of you will be, the picture is not pretty. You may already be flipping to the next chapter. My only saving grace in this formula is that I have large bones and can thus add 10 percent. My height is 73 inches (6'1") which, multiplied by 4, comes out to 292. Subtract 128 from that figure and I get 164 pounds. Now, Cooper says that if the circumference of my wrist measures 7 inches around (apply the same measure to your own wrist to see if you are "big-boned"), I get to add 10 percent of 164 (or 16.4 pounds) to the total. This comes to an ideal weight of about 180 pounds. If you are a woman you can determine large bone size by measuring wrist size to see if it is greater than 6½". If so, add 10 percent to your ideal weight.

My starting weight, beginning this volume, was 225 pounds. My conviction is that if a person is going to preach or write it, he ought to be doing his level best to live it. By any standard I was obese at over 45 pounds overweight. The following scales are a bit more generous, but even at that I was dangerously overweight. Also, notice that these charts assume you are weighing with 3–5 pounds of clothes on.

WOMEN Height	Small Frame	Med. Frame	Large Frame	MEN Height	Small Frame	Med. Frame	Large Frame
4'10"	102-111	109-121	118-131	5'2"	128-134	131-141	138-150
4'11"	103-113	111-123	120-134	5'3"	130-136	133-143	140-153
5'0"	104-115	113-126	120-134	5'4"	132-138	135-145	142-156
5'1"	106-118	115-129	125-140	5'5"	134-140	137-148	144-160
5'2"	108-121	118-132	128-143	5'6"	136-142	139-151	148-164
5'3"	111-124	121-135	131-147	5'7"	138-145	142-154	149-168
5'4"	114-127	124-138	134-151	5'8"	140-148	145-157	152-172
5'5"	117-130	127-141	137-155	5'9"	142-151	148-160	155-176
5'6"	120-133	130-144	140-159	5'10"	144-154	151-163	158-180
5'7"	123-136	133-147	143-163	5'11"	146-157	154-166	161-184
5'8"	126-139	136-150	146-167	6'0"	149-160	157-170	164-188
5'9"	129-142	139-153	149-170	6'1"	152-164	160-174	168-192
5'10"	132-145	142-156	152-173	6'2"	155-168	164-178	172-197
5'11"	135-148	145-159	155-176	6'3"	158-172	167-182	176-202
6'0"	138-151	148-162	158-179	6'4"	162-176	171-187	181-207

These weights are based on ages 25–59 based on figures of lowest mortality. Weight in pounds according to frame and indoor clothing weighing three pounds.

These weights are based on ages 25–29 based on figures of lowest mortality. Weight in pounds according to frame and indoor clothing weighing five pounds.

Notice I said *dangerously* overweight. A local hospital

newsletter recently reported that for every extra pound of body fat we carry, our hearts need to pump blood through an extra mile's worth of blood vessels. This, as we can imagine, puts an immense burden on our hearts. Furthermore, extra fat can increase our likelihood of:

- atherosclerosis (fatty deposits on the inner walls of the blood vessels)
- diabetes
- high blood pressure
- hypertension
- elevated cholesterol
- blood sugar imbalance

All of these put people at a greater risk for heart attack and stroke. Further, they contribute to lower energy levels, and frequently, a poorer self-image. Little wonder that Cooper suggests we "develop a healthy fear of obesity."[10] Says the researcher, "I'm becoming more and more convinced that obesity of any degree [including those 5 to 20 pounds over-weight!] can be a major contributing factor to all sorts of health problems, including serious coronary disease."

What about genetics? "I'm overweight because of the link between my genes and my obesity!" someone will undoubt-edly complain. Researcher Beth Newman recalls the days when people used to say that weight loss was a simple matter of will power and self-control. Then, with modern science and more sophisticated research they began to say that excessive weight might be due to genetic predisposition. "Now," says Newman, "the pendulum is swinging back again." Her stud-ies show that a good diet and proper exercise can help even those with certain genetic predispositions. "We don't deny that it is more difficult for some people to lose weight than others, but at the same time it is not hopeless." In sum, it may be harder for some of us to lose weight. But that is no excuse. We need to pursue a healthy body for a healthy total spirituality if we want to be all we were meant to be.[11]

The Danger of Going Overboard

Many men who spend an hour a day in physical exer-cises to keep fit refuse to spend an hour a week in the cultivation of their morals and their ethics. We have put so much stress on developing muscles and so little emphasis on developing our souls that our children are beginning to doubt if we have any souls at all (Allen E. Claxton).

Like all spiritual exercises, physical fitness is not a panacea! You can be physically healthy and be no where near the place in your Christian life where God would like to see you. In fact, Paul cautions that "physical training is of some value, but godliness has value for all things, holding promise for both the present life and the life to come" (1 Tim. 4:8). All I am saying in this chapter is that a little exercise, healthy eating habits, and weight control will have positive effects on almost everything you do in the pursuit of holiness.

You have been barraged with facts, figures, quotes, and research in this chapter. Perhaps it is mind-boggling. Let's simplify and get it down to four points to remember. Concerning overall fitness, the following recommendations are in order:

1. Begin exercising aerobically at least three times a week for twenty to thirty minutes.

2. Eat properly and responsibly three times a day.

3. Watch your weight; plan a lifestyle of exercising and eating that will help you maintain your ideal size.

4. Keep it all in perspective: we train our bodies physically in order to gain vitality in other essential Christian activities. It should never become an end in itself or the primary pillar of our spiritual quest.

Bulletin Board

The family is the first and essential cell of human society. (Pope John XXIII)

The Jew's home has rarely been his "castle." Throughout the ages it has been something far higher—his "sanctuary." *(The Book of Jewish Thoughts)*

I have never been given to envy . . . save for the envy I feel toward those people who have the ability to make a marriage work and endure happily. It's an art I have never been able to master. My record: five marriages, five divorces. In short, five failures. (J. Paul Getty)

The family can be the scene of wonderful affection and it can also be the scene of debasing friction. . . . Family solidarity takes hard work, much imagination and constant self-criticism on the part of all the members of the sacred circle. (Elton Trueblood)

CHAPTER SEVEN
Family

The following news item might be funny were it not so illustrative of many of today's families. Mr. Virgil Everhart wanted a divorce from wife Janet. He was slightly upset, but with full intention to divide things evenly Virgil took a chain saw to his Central City, Kentucky home and cut a six-inch gap through the flooring and walls for an even split. The Everhart home was torn asunder.[1]

That home in Kentucky is not the only one coming apart. The statistics and research of recent years point out some alarming trends. Increases in divorce, abuse, and a blatant disregard for traditional values are just a few of the disturbing developments. Christians are not immune to the malaise. If secular families are crumbling, we are beginning to find that the so-called "Christian family" is not much different.

Today, more than ever before, we need men and women willing to take a stand against the tide. Saints of former centuries who boldly opposed heresy were deemed *contra mundum* (against the world). It is certainly time for today's Christians to take a similar stand to counter the prevailing attitudes, conscious or subconscious, that combat the single most essential institution to both the kingdom of God and a wholesome society at large. We must stand in the gap and once again align our families with the purposes of God. In the next few pages we examine some crucial areas that will enhance the family for the kingdom of God.

Communication
In the thirteenth century Frederick the Great concocted an interesting experiment to determine man's "original language." Was there, he asked, a language native to man or are

infants destined to speak only the language to which they are exposed? He gathered a group of orphaned infants and instructed their caretakers to feed and clothe them but not to speak or interact with them. The Emperor eagerly awaited the exciting result.

He did not have to wait long. None of the children ever spoke; they all died within a very short time. Biologically, their needs seemed to be met. But the social deprivation was fatal. Evidently, this early attempt at a royal science project ended in disaster because a certain condition was not understood: little good happens without loving communication. That is as true in the modern family as it was in Frederick's day.[2]

Husband-and-wife communication

If you have ever flown on a commercial airline, the litany is familiar; with each departure a flight attendant recites the proper procedure in case of an emergency or loss of cabin pressure. "Place the mask over your nose and mouth," she drones, "and breathe normally." Though frequent fliers tend to tune out this interruption, the words that follow are critical if you are traveling with young ones: "If you're traveling with a child, please adjust the mask on yourself, and then on your child." The implication is clear. We will all breathe easier if the adults take care of themselves first and then move quickly to aid their children. Point number one of John Rosemond's "Six-Point Plan" for raising healthy and happy kids goes like this:

Pay more attention to your marriage than you do your children. In other words, put first things first and keep them there, where they belong and they are more likely to last. If you're a single parent, this translates: Pay slightly more attention to yourself than you do your children. Remember . . . you can't supply someone else's "warehouse" unless your own is fully stocked.[3]

Too many parents forget that. We can become so wrapped up in the daily demands of raising children and making a living that we forget we must attend to ourselves and communicate with each other *first* in order to effectively care for our kids.

The fact that marital communication is often neglected is no surprise to marriage counselors. In a study of 240 counseling agencies across the nation the question was asked, "What is the primary problem concerning marriage and family encountered by counselors?" Answer? *Communication,* plain and simple.[4] Wondering if I could confirm this with a friend who has his Ph.D. in psychology, I called with my question. "Phil? Just wondering, in the marriage counseling you do, what is the number one problem couples are facing?" "In the counseling that I do," answered Phil, "the biggest problem is, hands down, communication skills."

Socrates once stated, "I can think of no person to whom one talks less than his wife." Two millennia later J.R. Ewing, of the television series "Dallas," sneered to his wife Sue Ellen, "The less we have to say to each other, the better I'm gonna like it."[5] These statements from the famous and infamous are telling. Most men and many women could use some help in this area. Communication with our spouses frequently is not our strong suit.

In the womb men and women are differentiated in several ways which affect our whole approach to life and might help explain some of the difficulty.[6] One of the natural differences between the sexes is the inclination for verbal interaction. Girls, even immediately after birth, have more lip and mouth movement than boys. It is no wonder then that they talk earlier and with more sophisticated expression. In fact, a Harvard study involving preschoolers showed that in children's playground conversation, all of the sounds coming from female mouths were recognizable words. Sometimes the girls were talking to friends; frequently, they were talking to themselves! Only 60 percent of the output by the preschool boys was verbal. The rest were yells and sound effects like "Vrrroooom!" "Aaaaagh!" and "Toot, toot!"

This greater linguistic aptitude in the young ladies continues throughout life. There is no question that normally, adult women talk more than men. On the whole a woman speaks, for instance, about 25,000 words per day; the average man, 12,500 or about half. Gary Smalley notes that most wives admit needing about 45 minutes a day in meaningful conversation with their spouses. The men typically say that 15–20 minutes once or twice a week will do.

By any standard of excellence, 15–20 minutes spread out on an occasional basis over the week *will not do!* But I certainly can, from the male point of view, testify to the hard work and patience it takes to communicate meaningfully with my wife. One of my wife's gifts is the art of vocal loquacity. Simply, she talks a lot. Has since she emerged on that initial birth day. An early family joke purports that she was inoculated by a phonograph needle! And please do not think I am making fun of her. I *really do* consider her gifted. Because of her quantity of words our marriage is on stronger footing, our child is better educated, and the Friedeman household is rarely a dull place to spend one's leisure.

Being a typical male who needs 12,500 words or less a day, sometimes it flat wears me out. When I come home after one or two lectures and counseling with four or five students, besides a committee meeting and a discipleship group, I have spoken more than enough for one day. My allotment is used up! I sink into my easy chair and want no more. But — surprise! My wife is just getting started. After a day with our toddler she has only used up, let's say, half of her 25,000-word allotment. I do not want to talk; she does. On she goes as I grunt and pretend to listen. She wonders why I never remember anything she tells me; I wonder why she can't quit talking when I am reading the newspaper!

Gentlemen, get to work! Ladies, try to understand! We are different, and that means communication takes some emotional sweat and tender patience. A common debate in modern child-rearing goes something like this: which is more important — quality time or quantity time with our children? Whether time with children or conversation between spouses, there should be a *quantity of quality time!* And for most of us, that will probably mean a departure from the typical mode of behavior.

Of course, many other problems lie just below the surface in the communication game; to attribute all conflicts to natural tendencies would be unrealistic. But there are some general strategies that can enhance our interchanges. Below are a few recommendations for good spousal communication. Charlie Shedd hands the first two along; I add some thoughts of my own.

Recommendations for a Quantity of Quality Communication

Establish some sacred ground rules!

Spend at least fifteen minutes per day of uninterrupted, concentrated time listening to your spouse at the feeling level — not talking just about what you did that day, but also what you've been feeling. Share your victories, defeats, frustrations, hopes, dreams, disappointments, etc.

Spend additional significant time together each week. Have a date. Lunch, dinner, long walks — once a week or more if possible. Block out this time each week and hold it as a sacred trust.

Grab your spouse's hand and pray for your partner frequently. Ask that your spouse do the same for you. Make these prayers personal, specific, and conversational in nature.

Remember to talk often about the three major areas of conflict — money, sex, and in-laws. Be kind but frank, seeking solutions instead of placing blame. Communicate about these even if you don't think there is a problem. By the way, there will be conflict, and should be, for a healthy marriage. Some ground rules:

- Seek to change yourself, not your spouse.
- Agree on the subject and only tackle one at a time. Don't involve past conflicts or peripheral issues.
- Pick an appropriate time and place; in front of others, especially children, is the wrong place.
- Avoid unfair tactics like refusing to discuss and using the silent treatment, name calling, attacking areas of vulnerability (painful facts or other trusted personal information), raising your voice, using gestures that could be interpreted as a physical threat.
- Avoid dealing with symptoms rather than the essential problem.
- Finish the argument by coming to a solution or amicably postponing the fight until another time.

Evaluate yourselves. Are we effective communicators with

each other and our family? What could be improved? What are our assets in the area?

One way to conduct a communication checkup is by reading marriage books together. Two a year would be a good initial goal. Grab two different colors of ink pens, one for each spouse, and mark the sections of importance or interest to you; then hand the book back and forth. Use what you learn as fodder for future discussions.

A quick review for good spousal communication: Listen! Date! Pray! Fight constructively! Evaluate! Study together!

Parent-and-child communication

If communication between spouses is family problem number one, then you can imagine that high on the list of potential family conflict is poor communication with the children. One study I saw recently showed that middle-class men spend about thirty-seven seconds a day talking with their children. That piece of research stands as an illustration of the nonchalant communication style that all too easily emerges within the family. Like a marriage, relationships with children take work; communicating to them our love and acceptance requires intentional effort.

Merton and Irene Strommen suggest four aids to parent-youth communication. Although this research deals primarily with adolescents and their parents, the Strommens readily admit that each of these communication patterns has its roots early in family life.

Recognize the natural blocks to communication. Though present at every age, for adolescents these blocks might be described as growing self-consciousness, difficulty in describing feelings and emotions, and a growing resistance to authority. For younger children some blocks might include limited verbal skills, difficulty understanding adult concepts, and egocentrism.

At any age-level there are natural communication blocks. To communicate well the participants must acknowledge these and work around them as appropriate.

Take time to establish relationships. In the Strommen study, over half of the fathers, and nearly half of the mothers, spent very little time each day with their children! Further, one fourth of the ninth-graders spent less than five minutes on an average day alone with their fathers to talk, play, or just be together.

As with husbands and wives, a good quantity of quality time is needed to have maximum effect. When my wife was a youngster, her dad took each of his children on a monthly date—meal and event chosen by the honoree—just to be together. My favorite memories of my dad are the times he spent coaching my ball team or playing catch with me after noon meals.

Take the time!

Share thoughts and feelings. Parents need to verbalize their love, reveal their own weaknesses and struggles, and accept correction and insight when appropriate.

Children and youth need parents who can share their feelings and their frustrations. This makes adults more likely to listen, learn, and communicate love. It also makes them more approachable.

Focus on their concerns and interests. Parents need to focus on the concerns of their children and youth. Depending on the age of the child, these concerns could range anywhere from school performance to playground bullies to sex, drugs, and rock and roll.

Good communication focuses on the things that matter most to the one you are trying to love.

Good parent-child communication has two parts: talking and listening. Like the two wings of a plane, both are necessary. For instance, Dr. Burton L. White and his team of researchers noted that the amount of live language directed to a child (*not* television, radio, or overheard conversations) is vital to development of linguistic, intellectual, and social skills. Further, the best parents tended to be those who permitted their children to interrupt them for brief thirty-second episodes during which personal consultation, comfort, information, and enthusiasm were exchanged. Talking not only produced positive interaction in the present but laid the foundation for future development too.[7]

Listening, as might be suspected, is also critical, and a forgotten art. So what is a good listener? One study suggests the following:

- Listen without interrupting or being distracted by peripheral noises or events.
- Face the child squarely and look her directly in the eye. Maintain an alert and active demeanor.
- Listen for total meaning, detected not only by content but also by tone of voice, gestures, and other nonverbal cues.
- Listen to understand instead of to evaluate.
- Don't anticipate what is going to be said.[8]

Teach Them Diligently

God's words to Israel in Deuteronomy 6 are some of the most powerful found anywhere in Scripture. "Hear, O Israel," He thunders,

> The Lord is our God, the Lord is One! And you shall love the Lord your God with all your heart . . . soul . . . might. And these words, which I am commanding you today, shall be on your heart; and you shall teach them diligently to your sons (Deut. 6:4-7, NASB).

Those words "teach them diligently" are translated from the Hebrew *shanan* which is normally rendered "sharpen." Some linguists suggest that here, in the intensive form, it could mean "to incise, to carve into." The *New International Version* uses "impress." Whatever the translation, in Hebrew it is an unusual word that points out the intensity of the task. Carve, incise, impress the Word of God on the lives of your children! And just how was this to be done? God describes the means:

> You shall teach them diligently to your sons and shall talk of them when you sit in your house and when you walk by the way and when you lie down and when you rise up. And you shall bind them as a sign on your hand and they shall be as frontals on your forehead. And you shall write them on the doorposts of your house and on your gates (vv. 7-9, NASB).

In essence, says God, make My Word part of your every day.

Teach your children in the midst of your daily routine. That is the calling for parents today, as it was in the ancient Near East.

Faith
Marvin Wilson tells us that after the destruction of the temple in Jerusalem and the scattering of the Jewish nation into exile, rabbis began to refer to the home as a "small sanctuary" or "miniature temple." They taught that the home therefore was to be set aside for very special purposes. These included the worship of God (a "house of prayer"), the learning of the Torah (a "house of study"), and the serving of community needs (a "house of assembly"). One way that some of the rabbis helped comfort their people during the Roman destruction was to declare that the table in the home could and should take the place of the altar of the lost temple. The time of eating served more than a nutritional function; it was a means of religious service where the Torah could be taught by the priest (the father), songs sung in praise of God, and significant rites celebrated in remembrance of the holidays and feasts of Israel.

The contemporary Christian family should regain this sense of sanctity. Our homes should be sanctuaries, dinner tables our altars, parents should once again be priests, and religion enjoyed first and foremost in the home. The rituals of daily family prayer and Bible study, shared songs, meals, play, and celebration should form the warp and woof of any family that wants to emulate the godly pattern described in Deuteronomy 6.

Affection
In a 1971 study of high school youth designed to determine factors in family disunity, the Strommens found that one factor outranked all others: "My father and mother do not get along with each other." Say the researchers, "This simple statement is our most powerful indicator of family disharmony. Where father and mother are at odds with each other, the whole family suffers. The children become psychological orphans. . . . Family closeness actually fortifies children with an inner resistance to the toxins of life."[9] Zig Ziglar often

recalls asking his son what he liked best about his dad. The boy thought a moment before replying, "The thing I like best about my dad is that he loves my mom."

Affection is critical! Parental love should be displayed in the content, tone, and timing of words; lots of tender touching and hugging. Consistent acts of loving, caring affirmation between parents and their children will greatly enhance family intimacy. And one more thing. Phrases like "I love you" and frequent hugs should not stop when the child graduates to adolescence. There is a special need for visible expressions of affection as children enter adolescence and adulthood. A warm and accepting climate in the home not only produces well-adjusted children, it also provides the best basis possible for teaching them about their own sexuality and relationships, and how they fit into a world confused about moral values.

One of the best outgrowths of accountability groups lies in the area of affection in family relationships. In my own group, we covenant together to do something special for our spouses on a weekly or monthly basis—candlelight dinner, flowers, dates, etc. As personal testimony let me say that reporting back the week after makes for a fun meeting! It would be hard for groups intent on maximizing the family to overdo activity like that. A note should probably be added here: many parents will find such affection and openness difficult if they were not raised in an environment that reflected those qualities. If these elements have not been part of your family history, begin today. As time goes on, you will find the "love habit" one of the best you ever formed!

Money/materialism
Archie Bunker said it first: "There's three great things that happen to a man in his lifetime. Buying a house . . . a car . . . and a new color TV. That's what America is all about."[10] Perhaps God devotes so much of Scripture to the topics of money and possessions because He knows how easy it is for us to end up like Archie.

The lessons about assets and liabilities, checkbooks and balance sheets are first learned in the family. Some parents, by their lack of intentional instruction, teach that finances are an unspiritual facet of life and of little importance in God's economy. Other families, however, are learning that earning and saving, spending and giving, are part of significant Christian education appropriately gained in the home. If the family is important to God, and our attitude toward possessions is as well, then we might conclude that the two belong together in kingdom education. It would be a shame to end up like Mr. Bunker, thinking that you owned many possessions, only to find out that it was really the possessions that owned you!

TV

I'm prejudiced. Years ago I threw out my television set. I had to—I was addicted. Leaving the set in my room would have been like leaving a six-pack of beer and a fifth of vodka on the kitchen counter in the home of an alcoholic. So, I destroyed the thing. A bumper sticker on my car cajoles its readers to "Kill Your Television." Harsh perhaps, but I think TV changes—indeed, is changing—your life, as studies are beginning to show. Christians need to ease up on television and begin taking their time into their own hands.

Søren Kierkegaard, the Danish existentialist, commented in his day that "there is a far greater need for total-abstaining societies which would not read newspapers than for ones which do not drink alcohol." If Kierkegaard were alive today, I am sure he would either add to or replace "newspapers" with TV. It is dangerous.

A Gannett documentary entitled "Shock Waves: Television in America" described some of the effects televised media can have on a group of families. Sociologists had conducted a study on the effects of television in a community in Canada. In 1971 this mountainous enclave had no sets; in 1972 the TV was introduced thanks to satellite disks; in 1973 (twelve months later) the sociologists could already document differences in the people's behavior. Before the advent of this technological advance, children played games on the streets and sidewalks of their neighborhoods, adults shared frequent social interaction, and participation in community affairs was high.

After television, there was a dramatic increase in violence, and child's play became more physically aggressive. Reading ability and creativity testing showed dramatic decreases. Community entertainment dropped sharply while individual entertainment rose. Participation in community affairs plummeted. These dismaying results are all too real when one looks at the difference between pre- and post-TV America.

A *USA Today* graphic showed recently that in 1957–58 the average time of television viewing per day per person was five hours eleven minutes. The figures for 1987–88 were even more disturbing — we watched six hours fifty-nine minutes. Incredible! Television quickly seized the American attention and never relinquished it. I don't think that I exaggerate when I say that our ability to love, care, and share within the family, church, and community has been significantly blunted with the advent of the television set.

Neil Postman examined the broad effects of the television culture in his book *Amusing Ourselves to Death*. In the foreword, he describes the different visions of how a people can be deprived. He contrasts George Orwell's *1984* with Thomas Huxley's *Brave New World*. Recognizing that Orwell's vision is the one that captured the Western world's imagination and fear, he proceeds to suggest why our anxieties were misplaced:

1984	Brave New World
• Orwell feared those who would ban books.	• Huxley feared there would be no reason to ban books for no one would want to read.
• Orwell feared those who would deprive us of information.	• Huxley feared so much information that we would be reduced to passivity and egoism.
• Orwell feared the truth would be concealed from us.	• Huxley feared the truth would be drowned in a sea of irrelevance.
• Orwell feared we would become a captive culture.	• Huxley feared we would become a trivial culture, preoccupied with meaninglessness.

- Orwell feared those who control by inflicting pain.

- Huxley feared those who control by inflicting pleasure.

- Orwell feared that what we hate will ruin us.

- Huxley feared that what we love will ruin us.[11]

Postman wrote his book based on the premise that Huxley, not Orwell, was right. I think Postman surmised correctly.

We need to be held accountable for television's effect on us. I understand that the effect is potentially positive; I do not know of any households where a positive impact is currently taking place. Television tends to draw families away from interaction with the Lord, with each other, and with the church. By and large, it gives us lamentable role models, presents a distorted, secular view of reality, and stunts the educational advance of the entire family—from preschooler to Grandma and Grandpa.

One of my colleagues led an accountability group where the issue of family time came up. His fellow members were lamenting that there were just not enough hours in the day to spend significant time with their families. My friend asked a simple question: "How much time do you spend watching the tube on a daily basis?" "Hmmm. Two hours. Maybe two and a half." And no time for the family! Most fathers do not spend two and a half hours per month with any individual child, but we have no problem spending that kind of time watching Bill Cosby and Roseanne Barr. An accountability group could make a couple of suggestions at this point, with implications for years to come. Maybe the choices could be reduced to two: One, throw it out! Two, monitor it and spend as much time viewing as Jesus would if He were watching it with you.

Overdoing the Family

One of my hometown friends phoned one summer day about a decade ago, when we were both still in college. He asked if I would take a U-Haul 200 miles to the new home of his parents, pick up his mom and their furniture, and bring them back home. Although I did not ask, I presumed my friend was just too embarrassed to be put into a situation where both parents would be present though splitting up. I went.

I was more than a quiet observer. If I am asked to travel six hours back and forth in a moving van, I want to ask a question or two–or twenty. This family had sponsored ball teams on which I had played, served me ice cream on hot summer nights, and ferried me to track meets when I couldn't find a ride. I was brokenhearted over the dissolution of the marriage, and I wanted some answers. Come to find out that the father had been playing around with a girl half his age (one of my high school classmates!). The mother had cancer and was taking custody of the junior high girl and the mentally impaired son.

I was angry. I was brokenhearted. I was confused. This fatherlike figure was having a mid-life crisis at the expense of his family. He was apparently unrepentant and unabashed about the whole thing. Here I was, sent to move out the vulnerable mother and children, so that he could carry on his adulterous comings and goings. And there he was, helping me load furniture and prepare for departure.

After packing the U-Haul we went to a hamburger joint before starting the long trip home. It was a strange experience. There we sat—mother and father, estranged and at opposite ends of the long table with the daughter, the handicapped son, and me in the middle. Jimmy, the little boy who was at times in his life prone to brilliance, was obviously confused at all of this. We all knew that it would be too much to expect him to stay quiet through the ordeal. His verbal outburst that day was most intriguing, however. While we were eating, he continually looked over at his dad and said, "Daddy, I love you. Daddy, I love you. Daddy, I love you." I was opposite Jimmy at the table, half wanting to pinch him to get him to stop, half wanting him to continue and make his daddy squirm. Both mother and father were visibly embarrassed at this uncontrollable and incessant outpouring of emotion. Eventually, Jimmy looked over at his mother and said, loud enough for the whole restaurant to hear, "Mom, do you think I'm overdoing it?" The mother, with tears in her eyes, very gently nodded up and down. Jimmy, undaunted, said, "Well, I think it's about time we started overdoing it with Daddy!"

I will never forget the memory of Jimmy, all gangly limbs

and innocent emotion, jumping from the car as we were almost ready to head home and away from his dad. He threw himself at his father, not wanting to let go, lest he never had the chance to grab hold again.

I wept for days.

It is time to start overdoing family. Overdoing "I love you's" and prayers and hugs and time together and laughing and crying. Thanks, Jimmy, for the reminder.

Bulletin Board

The Christian ideal, it is said, has not been tried and found wanting; it has been found difficult and left untried. (G.K. Chesterton)

Truly, at the day of judgment we shall not be examined by what we have read, but what we have done; not how well we have spoken, but how virtuously we have lived. (Thomas à Kempis)

As thou art in church or cell, that same frame of mind carry out into the world, into its turmoil and its fitfulness. (Meister Eckhart)

I am persuaded that religious people do not with sufficient seriousness count on God as an active factor in the affairs of the world. (Thomas Kelly)

Bunyan in his Holy War speaks of some little devils that got down into the cellar of Mansoul, and asked to be allowed to stay there, but Emmanuel said "No." God's salvation does not leave little devils in the cellar, it touches and cleanses the deepest recesses of the soul. (J. Baines Atkinson)

CHAPTER EIGHT
Daily Christian Living

It may have been one of the most profound lessons the master ever handed on to the protégé. "One thing to always remember about life, boy," the wise man said, jabbing a crooked finger on the adolescent's chest, "life is soooo daily." Daily indeed! It is the unspectacular thoughts, happenings, attitudes, feelings, that occur moment by moment in our everyday living which make up the vast portion of our Christianity. We must be victors in the midst of the ordinary if we are to live lives that please our extraordinary God.

You will probably recognize this bit of folk wisdom that speaks of how small acts determine our destinies.

> For want of a nail the shoe was lost;
> For want of a shoe the horse was lost;
> For want of a horse the rider was lost;
> For want of a rider the battle was lost;
> For want of a battle the kingdom was lost —
> And all for the want of a horseshoe nail.

Daily Christian living is all about "nails."

Daytimer Christianity
I proposed earlier that one indication of a person's Christianity lies in his checkbook. I have heard the same thing said about the "daytimer," that little notebook where one's day-to-day schedule of activities and appointments is recorded. Discover an individual's priorities for time usage, and you will get a glimpse of the relative importance of the kingdom of God. Are the scheduled activities mostly self-serving, or other- and God-oriented? Are attempts being made to redeem

the time for the Lord and His causes? Do we spend too much time in leisure? Too little? Are enough hours out of the day and week prioritized for the family? For church? For private devotion? Important considerations!

A poll of *Leadership* readers revealed that the most frequently mentioned difficulty of the ministry had to do with time demands. It was also a contributor to five other difficulties: stress, feelings of inadequacy, spiritual dryness, fear of failure, and loneliness/isolation. The respondents to the study were primarily professional clergy. My feeling, however, is that the results are probably indicative as well of the layperson seeking to be God's man or woman in the trenches of life. To be all we were meant to be means getting a grip on one of God's most precious gifts to us—time. When it is wasted and finally gone, the other chapters of this book are meaningless.

After the study of Scripture and the practice of prayer, the saints of God need to think long and hard about their time priorities. My wife and I are dealing with this right now. We have come to the realization that we are too busy to maximize our lives for the priorities we feel God has given to us. We have recently determined God's call to us as (1) personal lives of devotion and piety, (2) a strong Christian family, (3) our vocations as Christian educators. But even in the context of these "callings" some tough decisions must be made. When do I let my son Caleb interrupt my spiritual disciplines? When will saying no to career advancement better enable me to be the kind of husband and father God desires? When extracurricular activities like speaking at conventions or resourcing retreat weekends beckon, how will I choose to accept or reject such requests in light of my already established time priorities?

I doubt there are any hard and fast answers to such dilemmas. But accountability groups can, through love, provide correction, support, and guidance in light of biblical priorities and God's particular call on our lives. A small group usually helps me see with more clarity my lack of sensitivity to time stealers. Many things lurk behind the pillars of my life to rob me of my time and negatively skew my priorities. A quick and undoubtedly incomplete list:

- No objectives, no goals, no time taken for planning and organization.
- Forgetting about the spiritual importance of how I use my time.
- Television/other media.
- Other people and organizations that are good causes and easily make me feel guilty for not becoming involved.
- Sloth and laziness.

I have a real need for a group of people who will surround me and keep me accountable for tne effects of these time stealers. My group gives me impetus to plan, to see time from God's perspective, to guard my attitude and habits regarding the media, and focus my time constructively. They help me say yes to the things to which God has called me and affirm me in the necessary limits of that call, to order my time so that my family and I feel we are doing God's will in God's way. Recognizing time stealers and taking action to redeem time in positive ways puts me at ease to be God's person.

Staying on the Sunny Side of Relationships

I confessed to my accountability group not long ago that I held a long-term grudge against a colleague at work. This gentleman and I had seen our relationship dissolve into perfunctory greetings. My group prayed with me and then sent me out to have a heart-to-heart chat with this individual. By the next meeting, I was to report the outcome. The result of that challenge helped me resolve, through face-to-face encounter, a long-standing sore spot in my life. It also helped me feel better about my entire career as a teacher in the institution where I serve. It healed a relationship, it healed my professional life, it healed me.

If we were made relational beings by God, then it stands to reason that when relationships in our lives are out of whack, our whole lives are affected. It is vital that we move into the fragmented relationships of our lives and seek to be agents of redemption. This often requires humility and courage, a willingness to undergo pain and to love unconditionally. But these are the stuff of Christian relationships.

There are other areas of relational health beyond unresolved conflicts. Scripture teaches that Christians should refrain from overly critical, judgmental attitudes, from gossip, from foul language, and coarse joking. From the lips of practicing Christians should come uplifting, loving, encouraging, and joyous speech. Not that there isn't a time for constructive criticism and judgment of God's community.

But Jesus once said that the things that "come out of the mouth come from the heart" (Matt. 15:18). If our hearts are full of the Spirit, and hence the fruit of the Spirit, then our lips should sing of "love, joy, peace, patience, kindness, goodness, faithfulness, gentleness and self-control" (Gal. 5:22-23). In the theological circles in which I run, we often speak of "heart purity." I have found that you frequently do not have to go beyond a person's speech patterns to determine what his "heart health" is. The gossip and chronic complainer tell more than they perhaps wish to about the extent to which they have abandoned themselves to God.

On the other hand, there are few things more beautiful than Christians who speak from a Spirit-filled heart, have found a righteous order to their relationships, and who desire to be held accountable.

The Attitudes of the Accountable

Attitude is described in the dictionary as the way you carry yourself which indicates your mood or condition. It is, simply, the outward posture reflective of an inward reality. If your mind is troubled, your face, body movements, and eyes are usually a dead giveaway to your hurt. For this reason, it is important that loved ones ask essential questions about our inward realities.

- How are you feeling about your life this week? What are your pains? Joys? Are you excited? Anxious? Afraid? Angry?
- Has how you have felt lately been reflected (for good or ill) in the way you've acted this week? Are adjustments needed?
- Are you approaching life with an attitude of thanksgiving? Of joy?

Many times I have been asked about these items in my life. I have always been grateful. The query usually drives me to check the problem within myself, ask the Spirit's help, and change my public display. Larry King, the TV/radio interviewer, recalls walking around Miami's Joe Robbie Stadium with manager Tommy Lasorda before a spring training game. Lasorda, ever the vibrant personality, was introducing King to players and generally having a good time. Lasorda walked past Eddie Murray at first base and said, "Hey, Eddie, how you doing?" Murray replied simply, "OK." At that, Lasorda went wild. "OK? OK? Two million dollars a year. It's March. There ain't a cloud in the sky. You're standing there wearing a major league uniform. You're thirty-three years old, you're going to the Hall of Fame, and you're saying OK? You say, 'Great, Tommy!' " Murray, looking at Lasorda like he was a maniac, seemed at a loss for words. Lasorda tried again, "You say it: I feel great!" So Eddie started saying, "I feel great!"[1]

The Christian has better reasons than Murray to say, "I feel great!" We ought to start in with confessions and actions. I remember an evangelist saying that most Christians need to have their heart send a message to their face, "I'm saved! I'm saved!" For, the speaker reminded us, most of the world is saying, "You're going to have to look a lot more redeemed before we believe in your Redeemer."

That evangelist's words remind me of a crossword puzzle my wife found in *USA Today*. She needed a four-letter word for "righteous." Could not figure it out. When everything else was filled in, we discovered that the answer was "SMUG"! I wonder how many people, believers and nonbelievers, have a similar definition.

Another important facet of Christian living is our appearance. When I am trying to make the best impression possible for the Lord by my example and the integrity of my witness, I want to know if there is anything I am doing that might peeve people or make them less receptive to my message. Many times, I do little things that annoy others and am clueless unless someone gently confronts me.

When I was courting my wife Mary, one of my friends got me alone in his truck and said, "Matt, there's something I just have to tell you before you go to Mary's home for Christmas." I braced myself, waiting for a revelation that would rock me. "Matt," he admonished, "you just can't walk up to her parents dressed like you normally dress." I looked down at my attire. What could be wrong with the way I dressed? Faded blue jeans, a T-shirt with a hole in it, and canvas hightops were what I would wear to see the Queen of England, and it would surely be good enough for the parents of my soon-to-be bride. Well, to make a long story short, I was convinced in the next half hour that it would not be wise to dress in my normal fashion, and I was also given a lesson or two on table manners before we adjourned.

I laugh now at that encounter, but I appreciate the effort of my friend to teach an uncouth, unkempt university grad a couple things about etiquette. He did not want me to embarrass myself, and I appreciate his risking a piece or two of advice. The point is, are we willing to listen to others if they have input about courtesies, protocol, hygiene, habits, etc.? I know that I want to be that vulnerable. But I love the gentlemen in my accountability group too much to allow them to stub their toes on little things that might hinder their overall Christian witness, and I trust they love me just as much in return. Of course, a healthy dose of tact is helpful when on the giving end of such advice.

Reader's Digest reported that a rocket headed to Venus was well on its way when communication between the computer and the rocket misfired. The rocket began slipping off course. Emergency procedure called for relaying a command, through a little messenger that looked like a tiny hyphen or bar (-), that the rocket should not worry. But for some reason, the bar was missing, the rocket worried, the computer began sending erroneous course directions and eventually the $18,000,000 rocket had to be destroyed. A reporter later wrote that it was "a touching and, in an odd way, a human story. The rocket was primed for a 180,000,000-mile trip, and stumbled over something this - long."

Accountability groups might sometimes be prone to nitpick. But in defense of such occasional activity, sometimes our nitpicking is all about "hyphens" that really matter.

Power
A Louisiana reporter by the name of John Camp did a revealing documentary on Jimmy Swaggart after the minister's sex-

ual escapades were revealed to the public; even Swaggart said it was fair and objective. Later an interviewer asked Camp, "How could this all have happened to him?" Camp had a ready reply. "He [Swaggart] certainly had no one he could confide in. He was standing alone at the top."

Richard Dortch, Jim Bakker's right-hand man, testified openly of power abuse. Bakker's sexual transgressions, he implied, were only symptomatic of unchecked power.

I think most all of us struggle with power in one way or another, and for many of us the problem stems from the fact that we stand alone at the top of our worlds, with no one in whom to confide at a gut level. Independence is where many evangelical leaders have fallen in the past several years, and it is where we run the risk of tripping up without accountability. Not many of us have to deal with the massive power of a millionaire, a politician, or a TV celebrity. But all of us are powerful. We have the power to live or die, to make this choice or that, to think, feel, or do in various ways. And yes, that is power.

We also exert such choices over other people, in the way we treat them, allow them to function, and help or hinder them. Power, when understood in this manner, becomes very real in families, the workplace, churches, and relationships of all kinds. Power has the potential to effect great good in lives—also debilitating evil.

God is all-powerful, omnipotent. Man, made in His image, reflects a portion of this power. Not that we can do *all* that we please, but God does endow each of us with a certain sphere of influence over which to exercise control. Our use of that power bears fruit or thorns in the decisions that we make.

To shirk our responsibility here is to perhaps claim, as some have done in Christian history, powerlessness. Such a relinquishment of God's gift to us is sin. We need to accept the gift of power and use it for His glory—creatively, redemptively, for the salvation of God's people, worldly structures, the environment. To use that power to excess, however, is abuse and can destroy lives, personal and corporate relationships, and the potential good effect of power. Let's draw some contrasts.

The Right Use of Power	*The Wrong Use of Power*
The Godhead/Father, Son, and Holy Spirit: creative, redemptive, life-giving	**Satan and his angels:** destructive, death-giving
Abraham: setting out in faith; blessed to be a blessing; letting God make his name great (Gen. 12:1-8)	**People at Babel:** working to make their own name great (Gen. 11)
Joseph: the "greater power" having mercy on the former "greater power"; using influence to save a nation from hunger	**Joseph's brothers:** leaving a lesser power—little brother Joseph—for dead
David: a heart for God; repentance and turning back to God	**David:** conniving, lust, murder
John the Baptist: trumpeting God's will	**Herod:** trumpeting Herod's will
Jesus: placing His life in the Father's hands	**Judas:** taking God's plans into his own hands

The greater the power, it has been said, the greater the abuse. The counterpoint is that the greater the power and the greater the trust in God, the greater the good.

You could follow the right and wrong reflection of God's omnipotent image in mankind throughout Scripture. At every juncture there is a chance for right and wrong use of power. This is why President John Adams said that "power must never be trusted without a check." Accountability—to God and people—is part and parcel of the right use of power. The need for accountability is why we set up governments with checks and balances. It is why institutions have boards of directors. It is why there is a need today for associations like the Evangelical Council for Financial Accountability. It is why, in part, Christianity must be a *corporate* reality and why we need God. Accountability, and the intentional development of checks and balances in our lives, is a necessity.

Thomas Huxley once said that "except by saints the problem of power is finally insoluble." Saints living under the authority of God's Word, gathered together, and looking for the grace and infilling of the Spirit of God provide the context in which the power in our lives can be held in check. The correct use of power in the lives of Christians is thus dependent on our connection with the Creator of power and with other believers who are seeking a similar connection.

"All power is a trust," said Disraeli, Prime Minister of Great Britain. If from a Christian viewpoint we recognize that God is trusting us to appropriate power for use on behalf of His kingdom, then we will take the necessary steps to get in right relationship to Him and His body — the church.

With a small group that loves you and wants to support your gift of power for His purposes, ask these questions of yourself.

- Do you have any impure ambition? Describe your pure ambitions.
- Have you abused your power in relationships since we last met? How so? Has God allowed you to use power redemptively on behalf of people in your life?
- Have you shown favoritism toward the rich or powerful since we last met? How so?
- What are your biggest struggles in this area of your life? Your biggest victories?
- How can this group help you manage power in your life?

The Bottom Line: General Questions

What are you learning?

I once had a discipleship group leader who opened heart-to-heart discussions with an interesting question: "What special lesson does the Lord seem to be teaching you right now?" Quite a thought-provoker! It certainly is a good question to hold before us in our daily Christian living. When we learn, we grow. When we quit learning, we quit growing. Simple as that. I have found this question helpful in keeping me mindful of the lessons God may be using to mold me into His likeness.

When I took my first position out of graduate school I was excited about my work. I was able to teach, study for the next lecture presentation, and maintain a full schedule of preaching, seminars, and small group activity. This was, in my estimation, career heaven. I was doing all the things I had ever wanted to do. But, as with most institutional situations, the honeymoon lasted only a short while. Nothing earthshaking really, just small disenchantments here and there that began to pile up into a disgruntled mind-set with where I was and what I was doing. On top of it all I began to receive offers from other institutions, some which I greatly admired, to assume different roles in ministry. My friends would casually inquire: "What is the Lord teaching you?" I am glad they asked. It helped me identify that the Lord was honing my skills as a thinker and presenter of ideas, to see my role as just one of the cogs in an institutional wheel, to know that all organizations, Christian or not, have difficulties and personality conflicts. These conflicts provide occasion for significant individual and corporate growth when properly met head-on.

Knowing that the Lord must surely be using my position to teach me, and recognizing as well that wherever I might flee there are similar problems, I am grateful that I did not just leave because "the grass is greener over yonder." I am thankful now that the Lord teaches persistence and that He uses well-placed inquiry from brothers and sisters in the Lord. "What is the Lord teaching you?"

Open to the Spirit?

We should be continually open to God's leading, guiding, teaching, and infilling through the person of the Holy Spirit in everything we do. Driving down the freeway should become more than a maddening traffic-jammed ritual. It becomes the hour of the day that the Spirit of God talks with us about His plans in the world and our part in those designs. Difficulties at work become the Lord's way to teach about endurance in human relationships. Stuffing envelopes for the company mailing is time redeemed — we see God breaking through the rhythm of letters. We remain continually open, seeking His presence in all that we do. He purifies our minds, our emotions, our wills. He empowers us to be His witnesses in a world starved for Christian integrity. He teaches us in areas where we desperately need divine schooling. But the process is maximized only if we are open.

Lordship?

This book is testimony to the fact that God wants to have dominion over every facet of our lives. Have we truly allowed Him to be Lord of *all?* Is He Lord of our sexuality, our money, our time, our difficult relationships, our families?

In my office hangs a cross, rendered in calligraphy by my wife, that contains the following words by John Wesley. They are a daily inspiration for me:

> Aim at GOD in every thought, every word and work. Swerve not, in one motion of body or soul, from Him, thy mark and the prize of thy high calling. And let all that is in thee praise His holy name — every power and faculty of thy soul, in every degree, in every kind, and at every moment of thine existence.[2]

An English evangelist once declared, "The world has yet to see what God can do with a man wholly dedicated to Him." Dwight Moody heard that statement and said, "By the grace of God, I will be that man." Just as God used Moody's whole-hearted dedication to reach millions, so He is ready to use in mighty ways all who will give their lives fully to Him.

Jesus in Our Hearts

An eight-year-old walked up to the wise old pastor and said, "May I ask you something? You say that I oughta ask Jesus into my heart?"

"Yep," said that pastor. "That's what the sermon was all about today."

"Well," said the boy. "How big do you suppose Jesus is?"

"Reckon He'd be pretty big," replied the pastor. "He was a carpenter, you know."

"That's what I was thinkin'," said the eight-year-old. "If I were to ask Him into my heart, wouldn't He sorta stick out?"

The pastor didn't blink. "That's right, Son. He'd stick out all over your life!"

The obedient, Christ-centered life is indeed "sooooo daily!" And Jesus will stick out all over it.

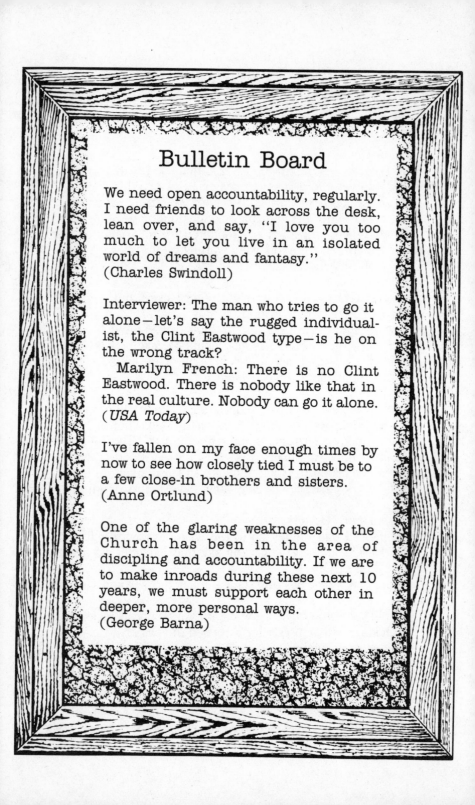

Bulletin Board

We need open accountability, regularly. I need friends to look across the desk, lean over, and say, "I love you too much to let you live in an isolated world of dreams and fantasy." (Charles Swindoll)

Interviewer: The man who tries to go it alone—let's say the rugged individualist, the Clint Eastwood type—is he on the wrong track?

Marilyn French: There is no Clint Eastwood. There is nobody like that in the real culture. Nobody can go it alone. (*USA Today*)

I've fallen on my face enough times by now to see how closely tied I must be to a few close-in brothers and sisters. (Anne Ortlund)

One of the glaring weaknesses of the Church has been in the area of discipling and accountability. If we are to make inroads during these next 10 years, we must support each other in deeper, more personal ways. (George Barna)

CHAPTER NINE

The Practice of Accountability

Alady convinced of the need for intimate community said to me recently, "Accountability, having a friend who is willing to spend time with me as we learn commitment together, has made all the difference in my life the last few months. I know I am at my best when I take my Bible and intimate relationships seriously." Exactly right! God does not intend for us to go it alone. Our earthly lives are too short and too eternally significant for us to think we can effectively imitate God's character and loving action without each other. We need each other to maximize our lives for Him.

Some Helpful Examples
The Christian faith has had many shining examples of saints who took accountability seriously in their pursuit of God. To highlight only a few is an unfortunate necessity here, but the following survey should provide us with a representative glimpse of healthy, supportive, accountable community interaction.

The early church
Karl Menninger in *Whatever Became of Sin?*[1] answers the question posed by the book's title by asserting that we ignored it, but it hasn't ignored us! Menninger notes, however, that if we have disregarded the human dilemma, the earliest of Christians refused to do so. They structured it into their gathering.

He recalls that the early Christian church cells were made up of small groups of people who met on a frequent—and often secret—basis. The order of worship was:

- self-disclosure and confession of sin, called exomologesis, followed by
- appropriate announcement of penance,
- pleas for forgiveness, and
- plans for making restitution, and finally
- a final period of friendly fellowship which would close the meeting.[2]

This general formula continued until the Council of Nicea, A.D. 325, says Menninger, when Constantine took over the church and replaced the requirement of open personal disclosure with private confession to a priest. From Constantine on, we got away from much of the spirit of the early years of the Christian faith.[3] Perhaps one of the most significant losses, however, was the small group confession, asking of forgiveness, and planning for restitution in the context of loving and caring community.

The Wesleyan revival

John Wesley is given much credit for reviving eighteenth-century England and inspiring a worldwide Methodist movement of heartwarming religion. Central to his method were small groups, which he actively promoted. His system of society, class, and band meetings provided a framework for spiritual nurture and accountable living. Although all the groups contained a degree of accountability, the band meetings were perhaps the most intense. Wesley drew up plans for the band meetings on Christmas Day, 1738 (the year of his evangelical conversion).[4]

The design of our meeting is, to obey that command of God, "Confess your faults one to another, and pray one for another, that ye may be healed." To this end, we intend, —

1. To meet once a week, at the least.
2. To come punctually at the hour appointed, without some extraordinary reason.
3. To begin (those of us who are present) exactly at the hour, with singing or prayer.
4. To speak each of us in order, freely and plainly, the

true state of our souls, with the faults we have committed in thought, word, or deed, and the temptations we have felt, since our last meeting.

5. To end every meeting with prayer, suited to the state of each person present.

6. To desire some person among us to speak his own state first, and then to ask the rest, in order, as many and as searching questions as may be, concerning their state, sins, and temptations.

Wesley proposed four questions to be asked at every meeting, others to be asked as often as the occasion might offer. The basic four:

- What known sins have you committed since our last meeting?
- What temptations have you met with?
- How were you delivered?
- What have you thought, said, or done, of which you doubt whether it be sin or not?

Other questions:

- Have you the forgiveness of your sins?
- Is the love of God shed abroad in your heart?
- Do you desire to be told of your faults?
- Do you desire that every one of us should tell you, from time to time, whatsoever is in his heart concerning you?
- Do you desire that, in doing this, we should come as close as possible, that we should cut to the quick, and search your heart from top to bottom?[5]

Tough questions! And we may feel that this methodology is simply *too* heavy. Perhaps, but Wesley's Methodists knew that if they were to do business with God and take sin on head to head, they must have not only the fullness of the Holy Spirit but also structure to help them maintain the heart purity they espoused. Sin, to the Wesleyans, was a growth restrictor and had to be dealt with head-on. A radical debilitator needed a radical cure.

Wesley Tracy states the following feelings about the questions of Wesley and then offers some contemporary alternatives:

These questions seem frightfully frontal and starkly negative to us. But remember, these topics were being discussed by openhearted friends who loved each other deeply. Further, if we restate these starter questions in today's language, we discover that they are extremely helpful to serious companions on the way to the New Jerusalem. I have used the following restatement of Wesley's questions successfully in several small-group settings.

1. Have you had any spiritual failures recently? Have you been disappointed with yourself lately, spiritually speaking? How can we be most helpful in restoring or supporting you? When we pray for and with you today, at what point should we focus our prayers?

2. What temptations or spiritual problems have you been battling lately? At what points in your life do you feel most vulnerable? Most weak right now? Most under pressure?

3. If you have been delivered from any temptations lately would you share with us how the victory was won? Would you share with us how you have endured and survived recent trials?

4. Has the Lord revealed anything to you about your heart and life that makes you want to take a prayerful second look at your attitudes, lifestyle, service, or motivations?

5. Is there a spiritual problem so deep or so personal that you have never been able to talk to anyone about it? Can you even talk with God about it? Are you carrying excess baggage from the past that still today keeps you defeated and depressed? Would you like to share it with us, your spiritual partners? Or, at least let us pray for you about it—would you set a time each day (or this week) when you are going to pray about this matter so we can at that very same hour pray for you wherever we are?[6]

Some Contemporary Models

Some people, recognizing the fundamental importance of interpersonal accountability, will go to any length to find someone to help them in their task of upright living. One young pastor travels 200 miles in order to enter into this kind of one-on-one community with an elder clergy colleague. Some people use regular weekly phone conversations that attempt to link life-to-life sharing and accountability. Letters can provide a measure of accountability. Some groups get together from all over the nation once a year; they devote a weekend in a hotel room to gut-level sharing and confession.

There are many possible models of accountability for the church today. But the best, by far, are groups that meet on a weekly basis to pursue holy living together. Explore the following models, and prayerfully consider which might be adapted to your context for accountability.

The Church of the Savior

The Church of the Savior has probably been among the more high-profile examples of accountability patterns in recent years. All members belong to one of several mission groups which consist of five to twelve persons. Through verbal or written reports, the participants in these mission groups share their spiritual progress in certain disciplines: daily prayer and Bible study, weekly worship and proportionate giving beginning with a 10-percent tithe of gross income. Other disciplines that are agreed on by the members of a group and are essential for the accomplishment of its peculiar mission may be included as well.[7]

Significant features of this model are: the basic disciplines are fundamental to membership in the church; members are held accountable for those disciplines in small groups; and the covenant of the small group disciplines is a means through which a missions objective is achieved in the surrounding community.

The model provides opportunity for entire churches to pursue holy living via challenging disciplines required for membership which are maintained through small group support, encouragement, and accountability. It is no wonder that The Church of the Savior has impacted its immediate culture far beyond what its membership numbers would suggest.

The Barnabas Foundation model
Dr. Allan Coppedge has successfully initiated accountability groups at Asbury Theological Seminary, using a pattern that has also been adapted in a small network of local churches. Coppedge's organization, The Barnabas Foundation, utilizes the small group model of discipleship and recognizes accountability as a vital link between theology and practice. At the beginning of each meeting, group members, under the direction of an understood covenant, report on their week of inner-life disciplines which include:

- A tithe of a "waking day" (a "waking day" equals twenty-four hours minus eight hours of sleep), or about an hour and forty minutes, in prayer and Bible study.
- Scripture memory—three verses.
- Fasting for a twenty-four-hour period.
- Attendance at public worship.
- Tithing.
- Weekly physical exercise.
- Daily family worship.

After these reports are given, the group director leads in a Bible study concerning discipleship principles and in a prayertime for the needs and concerns of those in the circle.

The Watson method
David Lowes Watson gives fresh expression to the Methodist heritage of accountability in his book *Accountable Discipleship.*[8] He suggests that an interested group of persons gather together and draw up a covenant of intent, highlighting agreed-upon disciplines. A sample Covenant follows.

A Sample Covenant of Discipleship

Knowing that Jesus Christ died that I might have eternal life,
I herewith pledge myself to be His disciple, holding nothing
back, but yielding all to the gracious initiatives of the Holy
Spirit. I faithfully pledge my time, my skills, my resources,
and my strength, to search out God's will for me, and to obey.

*I will obey the promptings of the Holy Spirit
to serve God and my neighbor.*

*I will heed the warnings of the Holy Spirit
not to sin against God and my neighbor.*

I will worship each Sunday unless prevented.

I will receive the Sacrament of Holy Communion each week.

I will pray each day, privately, and with my family or friends.

I will read and study the Scriptures each day.

*I will prayerfully care for my body and
for the world in which I live.*

*I will share in Christian fellowship each week where I
will be accountable for my discipleship.*

I make my commitment here, trusting in the grace of God to
work in me that I might have strength to keep this covenant.

Date:_____ Signed:_____

Watson suggests numerous optional clauses that could be inserted in addition to, or in place of, those already mentioned:

I will spend an hour each day with my children.

I will offer friendship each day to someone of an ethnic background different from my own.

I will witness to my faith in Christ at least once each day.

I will eat one less meal each day, and give the money to feed the hungry.

I will record the spiritual insights of my daily Bible reading.

When I am aware of injustice to others, I will not remain silent.

All members of the group should sign the covenant and carry a copy in their wallets or purses. Rotating leadership within the group, members share how successfully they upheld the various elements of the covenant during the week. Advice, guidance, encouragement, and correction are the order for the meetings.

Walk to Emmaus
Walk to Emmaus[9] is a spiritual life retreat program that not only allows participants to enjoy a meaningful and uplifting weekend experience but encourages them to engage in small group activity after their retreat activity is concluded. The eight-step program is clear and powerful and has been profitable to thousands.

Walk to Emmaus—ORDER OF THE REUNION

Come, Holy Spirit, fill the hearts of Your faithful and kindle in them the fire of Your love. Send forth Your Spirit and they shall be created. And You shall renew the face of the earth.

O, God, who by the light of the Holy Spirit did instruct the hearts of the faithful, grant that by the same Holy Spirit we may be truly wise and ever enjoy His consolations. Through Christ our Lord. Amen.

1. **Review Your Service Sheet**—They are to first share their "service sheet"—a program that includes disciplines for:

   (a) spirituality (morning devotions, prayer life, worship attendance, Communion, and spiritual retreat).
   (b) study (reading Scripture, daily spiritual guides, religious publications, denominational newspapers, religious magazines, attending Bible studies, church school classes, and religious seminars).
   (c) action (asking what have you done during the week so Christ will be better known in your: family, vocation, community, small group, Christian community).

2. **Closest to Christ**—At what moment this past week did you feel closest to Christ?

3. **Call to Discipleship**—At what moment during this week did you feel you were responding to God's call to be His disciple? Where did you participate in being the church this week, the heartbeat of Christ?

4. **Discipleship Denied**—When was your faith tested this week through failure?

5. **Your Plan**—What is your plan for spirituality, study, and action for the week to come? (see #1)

6. **Reunion Group Activities**—Talk about upcoming/on-

going mission/service projects and occasional joint recreational opportunities.

7. **Prayers for Special Needs** — Pray for those who may not have attended.

8. **Prayer of Thanksgiving** — Pray: "We give You thanks, Almighty God, for all the benefits You have bestowed on us. Who lives and reigns forever and ever. Amen."

The LifePlanner Approach

Paul Gray has meshed together the use of time management tools and spiritual growth features in a tool designed for the busy person in need of a personal organizer. Many similar systems help one to manage time and goals; the Life-Planner helps you to integrate spiritual discipline along with a time management system. I have used the LifePlanner for some time now, and have found that it has added enormous benefit to the organization of both my devotional and daily life. Inside of an 8.5″ by 5.5″ binder are color-coded, tabbed dividers that lead you to the following:

Christian Growth	*Time Management Tools*
Daily journaling and Bible study pages	Monthly, yearly, and five-year extended calendars
Goal setting in the following areas: personal, family, work, church, and community	Daily schedule with priorities and appointments
Topics of study for character development	Note-taking pages
Scripture memorization	Expense account log
Prayer diary	Telephone and address directories
Weekly, monthly, yearly spiritual growth analysis	

Ted Engstrom, author and President Emeritus of World Vision, says that "Everything I would look for in one bound volume to give me guidance for the day, month, year, and lifetime is found in this practical and compact planning guide. It is far more than a calendar, but rather a guide for living a life pleasing to God."

There is no question that I have profited from this tool. But I am just as excited about the group possibilities for the LifePlanner. An accountability group could share insights from journal entries and Bible studies, discuss progress toward stated goals in various areas of life and check Scripture memorization, etc. I have heard of some groups using it to beneficial effect. In fact, a group right now at the school where I teach isusing this plan. They each share their choice of a journal entry for the week and check each other's progress on their particular goals. While individuals study portions of the Scripture they want, at least one passage is studied personally during the week with the findings brought to the meeting and shared as a group. It's a good personal *and* group plan.

A group of folks could make significant spiritual progress with the LifePlanner as an organizing aid. For more information call 1-800-348-2513 or write LifePlanner, P.O. Box 535002, Indianapolis, Indiana 46253.

These are only a few historical and contemporary models. But all good accountability groups have this in common — each member gives the others permission to hold him accountable in his walk of discipleship. It is a place to grow in maturity, to share needs, to learn how to apply the Bible to daily living; most of all, it is a place to begin, in the context of loving community, to adjust our lives to biblical priorities in a wide range of areas.

We turn now to the pattern of accountability that I have devised and I hope will provide another good model for you to consider.

The "27:17 Model"

Out of the conviction that accountability is vital to Christian growth I have attempted, in the context of my own accountable relationships, to provide a profitable and practical model of small group discipleship. This model is named from Proverbs 27:17, "As iron sharpens iron, so one man sharpens another."

This design has been shaped by both the successes and the failures experienced in past accountability groups. I have sought to avoid two primary flaws. The first is spiritual myopia, a tendency of the group to be inward bound, developing selected devotional disciplines but neglecting intentional outreach as individuals and as a group. The second flaw is the failure to ask, and answer, pertinent and penetrating questions. It is all too easy to pray and study Scripture together but never reveal our true struggles. The "27:17 Model" includes a tool, in the form of specific questions, for examining the problem areas of our lives and together seeking God's solutions.

This model aims to provide a well-rounded approach to Christian discipleship within the context of an accountability group. The program includes three primary components:

Discipleship Covenant. This group covenant outlines the mutually agreed-upon purpose, goals, and commitments of the group, as well as establishing a format for the weekly meetings.

Accountability Inventory. These questions address the discipleship concerns discussed in chapters 2–8 of this handbook: development of the inner life, mission, money, sexuality, physical health, family, and daily Christian living. They provide a framework for growth as we search Scripture to determine God's perspective on these topics and systematically examine our lives to uncover shortcomings and affirm progress.

Action Steps. This component of the program provides the essential link between good intentions and spiritual growth. After each meeting we prayerfully consider what needs to be done to bring ourselves in line with the truth we have encountered—through God's Word, and by an honest appraisal of ourselves. Each member records a specific action to be taken and a timetable for achieving it. These self-determined steps are part of the next week's accountability.

This pattern has been tested and refined through hands-on use among the professors and students at Wesley Biblical Seminary, whose input has been invaluable, as well as at the local church level with men, women, and youth groups. Reproducible copies of the group Discipleship Covenant, Accountability Inventory, and Action Steps sheet, as well as Bible study suggestions for each of the accountability topics, are included in the Appendix. Following are practical steps for establishing an accountability group:

Step one. The first step is to identify interested individuals. Contact friends or acquaintances and, with covenant and accountability sheet in tow, explain the basic program. Significant accountability has begun when two or three gather with a common need and purpose. Accountability has power even in groups of two.

Step two. The second step is to establish the group covenant. Provide each member with a copy of the covenant sheet and work through it. First determine what you want to see happen in your lives. Perhaps everyone at the meeting could jot ideas on scrap paper and share these before trying to arrive at a synthesis. This is vital because, from the beginning, it gets the group on common ground and headed in the same direction. Even after the group is well underway, this statement is valuable in reaffirming your reason for being.

A group's goals usually determine whether it will be merely another nice gathering or one that is profoundly life-changing!

The remainder of the covenant sets down the functional necessities of the group: the time, place, and format of weekly meetings as well as individual and group disciplines. One very important consideration is the matter of duration (item 3). Always have a termination point for your group. If people know that there is a point of finality to their commitment, they are more apt to make that commitment and stick with it. Establishing a termination point does not mean that the group *must* disband, but it does allow people to drop out or move on without losing face. It also provides a natural opportunity for evaluating the group's progress.

For new groups, try covenanting together for a relatively short time—say, twelve weeks—in order to see if the methodology and the mix of personalities are a good match. A church could call the program "Twelve Weeks to a Changed Life." Use the Bible studies, the Inventory, the Action sheets, and Covenant together over that brief period. Cover one chapter in this book—and the corresponding category in the enclosed accountability inventory—per week. People willing to make the short-term commitment may discover that they want to continue. With the "27:17 Model" an initial time period shorter than twelve weeks makes it difficult to complete the Accountability Inventory.

Remember: the covenant is where we grant permission to other people to hold us accountable. It reflects our mutual commitment and aspirations. Because the terms of the covenant are derived from a cooperative rather than coercive process, I have found that in the "27:17 Model" individuals are open in their reflection and confession; rather than correction and rebuke, the group's function is encouragement and a joint effort to seek out solutions to our shortcomings. Vulnerability is an important component of the group process, and we should treat the confidences and confessions shared in our accountability groups as a sacred trust. But we should also be open to the honest input of others who are committed to our spiritual well-being.

Step three. The third step is to begin meeting. The format will be different for every group. A sample agenda might include:

- Gathering time (five minutes, snacks, light chatter).
- Prayer and possibly singing (ten minutes).
- Icebreaker (something light and interesting to get people talking) and then Bible study on the topic for the day, perhaps one of the major themes from the Accountability Inventory (thirty minutes).
- Sharing of the questions and "where we stand" on the items (thirty minutes).
- Development of Action Steps lists (ten minutes).
- Corporate prayer for empowering grace (five to fifteen minutes).

The Action steps are critical. It is not enough to say, "You know, guys, I'm really not doing that—and know I should be!" I often quote William James: "A difference that makes no difference is no difference." I would translate for accountability purposes, "A change of mind without a change of behavior means there wasn't a change of mind!" Accountability groups flounder in defeat if no practical guidelines are provided to help people make tangible headway in the cutting edge of life.

I have provided a sample Action Steps list in the Appendix. Many personal improvements in my own life over the past several months are the result of that sheet and the inspiration of my accountability group. There is power in setting down a clear, achievable, specific "to do" with a timetable and built-in accountability.

Step four. The fourth step is to evaluate the process. This should be done informally by the group leader, if there is one, on a continuing basis. "How is the group going for you?" and, "Are you pleased with the progress our crew is making?" are open-ended questions that should be asked outside the group time in order to keep tabs on the group's progress. Sometimes, as a result of such questions, small adjustments can be made that alleviate unnecessary discomfort and alienation along the way.

Formally, an evaluation sheet should be handed out at the group's termination point, addressing such questions as these:

- Are you interested in proceeding with the group or would you like a break?
- On a scale of 1–10 (1 = low; 10 = high), how would you rate this group?
- What needs did this group meet for you? What needs remain unmet?
- What were the strengths of this group?
- In what areas can this group improve?
- What one piece of advice would you hand on to the group if it decides to continue?
- Is the current method of accountability sound, or should we consider changing?
- What were the areas of greatest improvement in your life in the past several weeks/months as a result of this process?
- If you were to graph your spiritual growth over the life of this group, what would the graph look like?

The answers to these questions provide helpful information if your group continues and you want to improve it, or your group takes a break for a while or disbands, but you would like to try again with another group sometime. An evaluation process is only valuable if people are willing to adjust and adapt to make the next or continuing effort more profitable. And remember, a change in method is sometimes beneficial. There is nothing particularly sacred about any single approach. Stick with one long enough to find out how it works, and then evaluate whether you and your group should stay with that approach or find another.

Different uses of the "27:17 Model"

"27:17" groups may find that a category like "Mission" or "Health" or the "Inner Life" requires a month or more of meetings. Feel free to do as the group prefers. One leader told me that his group worked on only three categories over several months and planned to tackle the others later. Whatever you do, find a method for breaking the categories and meetings down into smaller bites. A few years ago I tried to tackle the whole thing all at once and just about blew my group's circuits. I found a poem that aptly describes what happened.

> The centipede was quite happy
> Until a frog in fun
> Said, "Pray, which leg goes after which?"
> That worked her mind to such a pitch
> She lay distracted in a ditch
> Considering how to run!

Other applications of the "27:17 Model" appear in the Appendix.

The Ups and Downs of Group Accountability

If a group of people genuinely wants to grow spiritually and will follow the guidelines and steps in this chapter, they can expect that:

- There will be an increasing Christlikeness in the participating individuals and in the accountable community. Further, an exciting sense of "koinonia" will develop as group members grow and help their friends grow in the Lord.
- A certain excitement begins to develop as the Christian walk becomes less theoretical and much more practical.
- Better employees, more loving and effective husbands, wives, and parents are developed, responsible lay and clergy are stimulated to holy living, and people of all walks are changed—thereby becoming change agents of God's kingdom.
- Disciples of Christ are reproduced.

Simply, the small group accountability model—appropriately applied—is one of the best means of grace available for persons desiring to be all that God wants them to be.

The "27:17 Model" has had some exciting results. One group leader reported that it got his discipleship group off with a *bang!* He explained: "Most groups I have led in the past have taken three-fourths of a year to finally get to the place where we can share anything significant or revealing about our lives. This inventory had us making progress immediately!" Other comments:

I deal with college-age kids. They need to go through questions like these to think about where we are and where we *can* go. There are specific questions for specific areas. You're not just guessing. It gives you a measuring device about how you are doing! (associate pastor)

It has been a good springboard to get my ladies to think, feel, and make crucial changes in their lives. (discipleship group leader)

We have used it so much that my guys know the questions by heart. Occasionally, I check back just to make sure we are still covering all the bases. But it has been just great. (Christian Education director)

It's wonderful. It helps me evaluate my own life and recognize where my strengths and weaknesses lie and then get to strengthening my weaknesses. I'm learning about commitment from my group. It helps me see Bible truths in many areas of my life that I've never really thought about before. (laywoman)

I've had several discipleship groups through the years. I was excited by how much more quickly the group gelled because of the "27:17" questions. The use of the instrument broke down the normal barriers. On some of the topics we spent several weeks—especially on the tough topics like money and sex. The Action Steps have led to real change. (seminary professor)

There are potential pitfalls, and knowing about them in advance will keep your group from tripping up.

Works righteousness

The accountability process described in the "27:17 Model" can, without an intentional attitude of humility and grace, develop into mere performance that tries to impress others or put oneself in God's good graces. It can, sadly, become a kind of works righteousness. Elizabeth O'Connor reminds us:

> We would warn against the disciplines becoming another form of perfectionism, a holy rule by which one is self-justified. The discipline is a response to the waiting grace of God. It helps keep us open to the love of God. It helps keep our feet upon the pilgrim way. He who becomes self-righteous has wrongly conceived the meaning of the disciplines. Day by day the disciplines let us see ourselves against the agape love of the cross, and when we thus see ourselves we are led to humility, not pride.[10]

In the process of accountability, one cannot overemphasize humility. We should be more quick to identify our own faults than the shortcomings of others. And love should be our motive for any suggestions or corrections. Martin Luther King was right when he noted that "whom you would change, you must first love." Change in the context of love is the most enduring and the most effective in the long haul. Humility and love are crucial to a successful accountability group.

Authoritarianism

A second danger is that of taking an authoritarian approach rather than treating the group as family. In recent years accountability has been given a bad name by some Christian movements because of the issue of control. What the person in authority said, subordinates did. Simple enough. But wholesale control is dangerous, and lives are more likely damaged than maximized for God's kingdom. The spiritual accountability I promote consists of individuals granting others permission to probe, correct, and check up on spiritual progress. It is *not* committing to a "blank check" subordination.

Recently the Rev. Bob Mumford, a key leader in the charismatic shepherding movement that grew to over a million followers, publicly apologized for the cult-like direction of the groups. The shepherding movement began, evidently, as an attempt to address a lack of discipline among members of "Spirit-filled" churches. Said Mumford, "People took something that began in the Spirit and attempted to perfect it in the flesh." The attitude became, "I'm going to help you walk straight, even if I have to coerce you." In retrospect, Mumford said simply, "This is not the spirit of the Gospel."[11] As mentioned in the opening chapters, accountability in community is liberating, broadening, freeing. It is not coercive, fleshly, cult-like.

We are called to seek the accountability of those who love and care for us, but remembering to keep our thinking caps on when we do so.

Burnout
A third danger is burnout. The accountability process can be so intense that people get weary and quit. As previously mentioned, a termination and reevaluation date is one antidote to burnout. So are liberal doses of laughter, joy, and encouragement. Where these elements are lacking, take note, and include them. They are necessary for enduring relationships. Do not burn out because of a dearth of joy.

A.C. Quigley used to be a basketball referee, among other roles, for the Kansas Jayhawks. He had an unorthodox way of letting players know they had fouled. He would rush up to them, point a long, stringy finger in their face, and shout "YOU CAN'T DOOOO THAT!" They got the message! I hope that people in accountability groups do not take a similar approach, however. If they do—believe me—the process will crumble and crash.

For whatever it is worth, I have been in groups that lacked both a termination point and the liberal amounts of lightheartedness, and not only did we burn out, some of us left angry and disillusioned. How sad! Such finales can be easily avoided.

Perseverance

A fourth danger—giving up on the concept of accountability because of particular difficulties that might arise. Ron Sider, author and professor, reflects on his own efforts at accountability and says that one of the keys to this kind of community is perseverance. "We should not give up working on it," he says. It is too important. As one would-be poet put it:

> To dwell above, with saints we love,
> That will be grace and glory.
> To dwell below with saints we know,
> That's another story!

It certainly is not easy. But as John Wesley claimed, there is no Christianity without this kind of working, intense, community discipleship.

Personality-based Structure

I think it is important to remember that just because the inventory has numbered items in neat rows, the process does not have to be highly structured. Many personality types are in no way given to the high structure needs of other types. Reginald Johnson discusses four small group models, based on the four typologies of the Myers-Briggs Temperament Analysis; all can be used with the "27:17" Inventory:

- Covenant-Discipleship Model: write a covenant, specify the minimum disciplines, set and meet goals, regular evaluation. (Sensing Types)
- Bible Study Group: makes use of personal study, lecture, discussion, note-taking, individual reports. (Thinking Types)
- Prayer and Sharing Group: focuses on building of friendships, intercessory prayer, strengthening group trust, informal discussion. (Feeling Types)
- Great Christian Books Group: read and discuss classics and share ideas and inspirations. (Intuitive Types)

The Spirit's Tool

Finally, there is the danger of thinking that an accountability group can be the primary means of leading an individual to a pure heart and Christian maturity. It can never be such an agent of change. That can only be done by the Holy Spirit. Probing and querying each other can be one means—and a powerful one at that—used by the Spirit. But it must nonetheless be seen as a means and *not* the cleansing agent itself.

Dangers always dog worthwhile endeavors. So it is with accountability. But we should not be deterred. Because deadly mishaps happen in cars does not mean I quit driving. Because abuse happens in the home does not mean I quit disciplining my children. Because the Bible was once used to defend racism does not mean I turn my back on God's Word. And just because accountability has been abused in the past or has been found to have dangers does not mean I neglect it as a necessary means of grace. This biblical theme of discipleship and accountability has been a constant throughout Christian history in individual and corporate renewal, and is certainly applicable to modern disciples as well.

In writing this book I have often pictured Moses on the hilltop as the Israelites encountered the unfriendly Amalekites. "Choose some of our men and go out to fight the Amalekites," he instructed. "Tomorrow I will stand on top of the hill with the staff of God in my hands" (Ex. 17:9). Joshua led the battle charge; Moses and his "men"—Aaron and Hur—would stand at the top of the hill to watch the battle. But an interesting dynamic accompanied the fight.

> As long as Moses held up his hands, the Israelites were winning, but whenever he lowered his hands, the Amalekites were winning. When Moses' hands grew tired, they took a stone and put it under him and he sat on it. Aaron and Hur held his hands up—one on one side, one on the other—so that his hands remained steady till sunset. So Joshua overcame the Amalekite army with the sword (vv. 11-13).

This is a picture that the Christian must remember. To be all that we were meant to be, we need others. Those who will encourage, exhort, rebuke. Those who will place a foundation of stone under us and hold up our hands when we are weary. That is what accountability is all about.

A NOTE FROM THE AUTHOR

If this volume has been helpful to you and/or you end up putting an accountability group together, I would love to hear from you. My address:

Matt Friedeman
P.O. Box 9938
Jackson, Mississippi 39286

(601) 362-1305

May God Bless!

Appendix A

Ideas for Use of the "27:17 Model"

Launch a church-wide program. Advertise a program of short duration such as "12 Weeks That Will Change Your Life" to kick off some groups in your church. Train some leaders in the process adapted to your church and implement the program. At the end of the twelve weeks, see if anybody wants to continue this or a similar type of group. This process could be offered on an ongoing basis in a church with accountability groups sprouting up all the time in response to a continuing emphasis.

Maximize your personality type. Discover a way that the "27:17" Inventory could aid one of the four models below:
- *Covenant-Discipleship Model: write a covenant, specify the minimum disciplines, set and meet goals, regular evaluation. (Sensing Types)*

- *Bible Study Group: make use of personal study, lecture, discussion, note-taking, individual reports. (Thinking Types)*

- *Prayer and Sharing Group: focus on building of friendships, intercessory prayer, strengthening group trust, informal discussion. (Feeling Types)*

- *Great Christian Books Group: read and discuss classics and share ideas and inspirations. (Intuitive Types)*

Try a category per week. Deal with one or two questions in depth in each category for several weeks and then go back to the first category and start over, taking one or two more questions from each category. Don't be afraid to review them to be sure that you are continuing to grow in each area.

Try another model. After the group is satisfied that all the areas have been covered adequately, go on to another method of accountability and refer back to the "27:17 Model" on a regular (monthly, semiannually, yearly) and scheduled basis.

Plan a retreat. Use a particular category of questions for a spiritual life retreat. Depending on the length of the retreat, take a category per day, or half day, and develop your program around them.

Personalize the questions. For a month or so, choose and circle the questions out of the entire Inventory you would like the group to ask you at meetings and hold you accountable for. In this method be sure to make heavy use of the "to do" sheets.

Go deep in one category. Let's say you want a group that specifically addresses improving relationships within the family units represented. Go to the family questions, beef them up, add some more, and then focus on those questions for several weeks.

Maybe a few pastors in town want to be held accountable for numerical growth in their churches. Develop a whole new category and covenant together for progress.

Try a private study. Use the Inventory in your devotional time, praying over the questions and studying Scripture in each area on a one-category-a-day basis.

Steps to Consider in Beginning a "27:17" Accountability Group

1. Pray that the Lord will lay on your heart a few people to challenge to the small group process of accountability and spiritual growth.

2. Get a small group (three to six) together and fill out the Covenant sheet.

3. Assign several Scriptures in a certain category to study before the weekly meeting. At the meeting, look those over together and raise questions about the passage to stimulate discussion. Begin with "Issues" as an introductory category, and move through the rest in the order the group desires.

4. Meet and take turns sharing from your own experience your answers to the questions for each category—victories and struggles—and suggestions for self-improvement.

5. Fill out your Action Steps list weekly and report your progress at the next meeting. Make the action specific, measurable, and achievable, and include a completion date or timetable.

6. Make prayer and continual encouragement key elements of your meeting.

7. Repeat the process weekly for twelve weeks and then disband or regroup, as the Lord leads.

Appendix B

Accountability Inventory

The following questions are meant to be used in a small group setting to encourage an accountable lifestyle and righteous change in behavior. They may be reproduced for class use only.

Chapter 2 Bible Study/Resource Suggestions

Below are suggestions for individuals or small groups who would like to study devotional life further. Members of a small group may study some of the Scripture passages prior to the group meeting and share their insights upon convening. Two methods of Bible study are described in Appendix E.

Devotional Life Study Passages/Questions:

Genesis 2:7 The Old Testament word here for "breathed" is the same word for "wind" and "spirit." What is the connection between God's breath/wind/Spirit and life? See also Ezekiel 37:1-14 and Acts 2:1-4.

Psalm 119:9-16 How many spiritual disciplines can you pick out in this passage, and how do they help us seek Him with all our hearts?

Matthew 6:16-18 How are the spiritual disciplines supposed to be practiced?

Matthew 7:21-23 What does it mean and what is involved to know, and be known by, God?

Mark 7:1-23 What are the lessons here concerning outward traditions and the heart?

Mark 1:35-38 What is the link between prayer and action?

Luke 6:12-16 What is the link between prayer, discernment, and relationships?

John 15:1-8   What are the practical implications for spiritual growth from this passage?

Acts 1:4, 12–2:4   What did it mean here to "wait"? What were these disciples doing while waiting?

Romans 12:1-2   What are the full meanings of "conform" and "transform"?

Revelation 3:14-22   Are any characteristics of this church true of your church, or you personally? What are the antidotes?

Other Resources to Consider:
Ordering Your Private World by Gordon MacDonald
Celebrate My Soul by Reginald Johnson

Accountability Inventory

Devotional Life: Questions to consider...
1. Are you praying and studying Scripture daily? How much time do you spend each day?
2. Are you approaching Scripture "formationally" as well as "informationally"? Are you praying to "align" your life with His and not just to get something from God?
3. What good Christian books have you been reading since we last met? What important lessons are you learning?
4. What other inner life disciplines have you been trying? What has been the effect? Have you found an effective personal growth mix?
5. Have you fully surrendered yourself to God and His will without reservation? Have you allowed the Spirit to "be loosed" into the entirety of your life?

6. What are your biggest struggles in this area of your life? Your biggest victories?

Chapter 3 Bible Study/Resource Suggestions

Below are suggestions for individuals or small groups who would like to study mission further. Members of a small group may study some of the Scripture passages prior to the group meeting and share their insights upon convening. Two methods of Bible study are described in Appendix E.

Mission Study Passages/Questions:
Genesis 12 Abraham was blessed to be a blessing — what implications are there for our lives today?

Ezekiel 16:49-50 Name the sins of Sodom. How do those sins affect a city, a nation, a person?

Matthew 5:13-16 What are the properties of salt and light? How is the believer to reflect those qualities?

Matthew 9:35-38 How did Jesus respond to the needs of others? What did/does He command His disciples to do?

Matthew 10:32-42 What prospects does Jesus offer His disciples in this passage? Why do you think He included this message?

Matthew 25:31-46 What actions characterize the "good and faithful servant"? (vv. 21, 23) When have you participated in the ministries of mercy Jesus mentions?

Matthew 28:16-20 What are the characteristics of a disciple? How are disciples made?

Luke 4:14-21 According to Jesus, to whom was He called to minister? How was this demonstrated in his life? What priorities does this suggest for your own outreach?

Luke 10:30-37 What qualities did the Good Samaritan possess that the other potential helpers did not?

Acts 2:42-47 Compare this passage with Acts 4:32-37. How

did the early church's ministry reflect Jesus' priorities?

Ephesians 4:7-16 What gifts has God given the church? For what purpose?

James 1:27; 2:14-17 How does this "good religion" differ from what many consider to be "good religion"?

1 John 3:16-18 What are the implications for the "love of God" in our lives?

Other Resources to Consider:
Unleashing the Church by Frank Tillapaugh
Life-Style Evangelism by Joe Aldrich
The Master's Plan for Making Disciples by Charles Arn and Win Arn
The Mustard Seed Conspiracy by Tom Sine
In His Steps by Charles Sheldon

Accountability Inventory

Mission: Questions to consider . . .
1. Are you personally involved in a regular, intentional way to spread the Good News to your friends, relatives, associates, and neighbors?
2. Are you personally involved in a regular, programmatic way to serve the poor and needy?
3. Have you been able to establish your vocation as a mission field for the Lord? What steps have you taken (are you taking)?
4. Are you developing and nurturing a vision for world outreach? How?
5. What are the biggest struggles in this area of your life? Your biggest victories?
6. How could this group enable you to be about God's mission in the world today?

Chapter 4 Bible Study/Resource Suggestions

Below are suggestions for individuals or small groups who would like to study money further. Members of a small group may study some of the Scripture passages prior to the group meeting and share their insights upon convening. Two methods of Bible study are described in Appendix E.

Money Study Passages/Questions:
Genesis 14:17-20 Abraham is the first recorded tither in the Bible. What was his motivation? Remember, this was pre-Mosaic Law!

Deuteronomy 14:22-29 The tithe in Mosaic Law was for what use? Any implications for giving patterns?

Malachi 3:8-12 What challenge does God issue in this passage?

Matthew 6:19-21 What are treasures in heaven? Treasures on earth?

Matthew 6:25-34 How does faith in God reduce our worry? In the context of these passages, what does it mean to seek first the kingdom of God and His righteousness?

Matthew 23:23-24 What danger of tithing does Jesus suggest here?

Mark 10:17-31 Why is it hard for the rich to follow Jesus?

Luke 21:1-4 By what standards does God judge our gifts?

2 Corinthians 9:6-15 What are the benefits of being a cheerful giver? What keeps us from such generosity?

Other Resources to Consider:
Rich Christians in an Age of Hunger by Ron Sider
Money Matters by Ron Blue
Answers to Your Family's Financial Questions by Larry Burkett

Living More with Less by Doris Janzen Longacre

Accountability Inventory

Money: Questions to consider . . .
1. Have you developed a personal budget with your family yet?
2. Are you out of debt, or making significant progress toward that end?
3. Have you explored ways to decrease your expenses in order to have more discretionary money?
4. How are you combating materialism?
5. Are you seeking ways to increase your regular and special giving to the Lord's work?
6. Are you saving for future needs?
7. What are the biggest struggles in this area of your life? Your biggest victories?

Chapter 5 Bible Study/Resource Suggestions

Below are suggestions for individuals or small groups who would like to study sex further. Members of a small group may study some of the Scripture passages prior to the group meeting and share their insights upon convening. Two methods of Bible study are described in Appendix E.

Sex Study Passages/Questions:
Genesis 39   How did Joseph respond to sexual enticement? What reasons did he give for his conduct?

Exodus 20:14   Why is adultery a sin against God?

Song of Songs 8:6-7   Why do you think this book—with its highly sensual character—is included in the Bible? What message does it have for us?

Matthew 5:27-30   Why does Jesus use hyperbole on this point of adultery?

1 Corinthians 5   What is Paul's response to sexual immorality among believers?

1 Corinthians 6:13-20   According to Paul, what is the Christian's motivation for sexual purity?

1 Corinthians 7:1-9   Why does Paul spend this much time on such personal subjects? What are his main points?

Ephesians 5:3-5   What types of activities does Paul name as impure and unsuitable for the Christian? In your workplace and social life, from which do you need to guard yourself?

Other Resources to Consider:
Bonding by Donald Joy
Unfinished Business by Donald Joy (for men)
Intended for Pleasure: Sex Techniques and Sexual Fulfillment in Christian Marriage by Ed and Gaye Wheat
Money, Sex, and Power by Richard Foster

Husbands and Wives by Hendricks and Neff
Sex and the Single Christian by Audrey Beslow

Accountability Inventory

Sex: Questions to consider . . .

1. What temptations concerning your sexuality have been particularly difficult since we last met?
2. (if married) Are you taking steps to develop an increasing intimacy with your spouse? What special gesture or gift have you done for, or given to, your mate since we last met? Are you spending significant amounts of time talking with him/her on a daily basis?
3. (if dating) Are you taking steps to develop an increasing intimacy with your friends of the opposite sex while maintaining abstinence sexually? Are you moving slowly with the physical aspect of your relationship?
4. Is there a relationship or emotional attachment with a member of the opposite sex that could be potentially dangerous? What is the danger?
5. Have your thoughts been free from lustful temptation and daydreaming? Are you watching or listening to any product of the media which stirs up problems with lustful thought?
6. What are some hidden events from the past that affect your sexual purity today? What clues would relationships with your father, mother, siblings, or intimate others give us to help us deal with current successes and failures with your sexuality?
7. What are your biggest struggles in this area of your life? Your biggest victories?

Chapter 6 Bible Study/Resource Suggestions

Below are suggestions for individuals or small groups who would like to study health further. Members of a small group may study some of the Scripture passages prior to the group meeting and share their insights upon convening. Two methods of Bible study are described in Appendix E.

Health Study Passages/Questions:
Proverbs 23:1-3 Guard your appetite.

Daniel 1:3-17 How did Daniel respond when offered a life of indulgence? Why? What was the result of his "alternative lifestyle"?

1 Corinthians 6:12-13, 19-20 In this passage, what principles do you see for establishing a healthy lifestyle?

1 Timothy 4:7-8 We often diet and exercise for appearance's sake. What should be the Christian's motivation for pursuing good health?

Other Resources to Consider:
The Aerobics Program for Total Well-Being by Kenneth Cooper
American Heart Association: pamphlets on nutrition, exercise, and aerobic activity that are free and helpful. Go to your local center for information.

Accountability Inventory

Health: Questions to consider . . .

1. Have you participated in some kind of aerobic activity at least three times this week?
2. Is your weight within five pounds of what is recommended? If not, are you taking steps to rectify the situation?
3. Do you have a healthy, responsible diet? Are your eating habits healthy?

4. Have you had a regular checkup from the doctor this year? Are there recommendations you need to be following?
5. What are your biggest struggles in this area of your life? Your biggest victories?

Chapter 7 Bible Study/Resource Suggestions

Below are suggestions for individuals or small groups who would like to study family further. Members of a small group may study some of the Scripture passages prior to the group meeting and share their insights upon convening. Two methods of Bible study are described in Appendix E.

Family Study Passages/Questions:
Deuteronomy 6:1-9 What is God's command to parents? Where should they teach? How can you apply these verses to your own family situation?

Joshua 24:14-15 In Joshua's day, what things competed for the devotion of the people? What things grab your family's time and attention today? How are you "choosing this day" on these issues?

Ephesians 5:22–6:4 What is Paul's primary instruction to wives? To husbands? Children? Parents? What is to be the motivation in all family relationships? (vv. 1-21)

1 Corinthians 13 What does this love look like from a parent? Husband? Wife?

Colossians 3:18-21 Submit, love, obey, do not provoke: what are the fuller meanings of these words and their implications for the family?

1 Timothy 3:2-12 What family relationships are depicted in this passage? How does family life impact one's ability to minister effectively? Compare Titus 1:6-9.

Other Resources to Consider
Love for a Lifetime by James Dobson
Husbands and Wives by Hendricks and Neff
Parents and Children by Kesler, Beers, and Neff
Parents and Teenagers by Kesler and Beers
Raising Positive Kids in a Negative World by Zig Ziglar
Living, Loving, Leading by David and Karen Mains

184 THE ACCOUNTABILITY CONNECTION

Accountability Inventory

Family: Questions to consider...

1. Have you maintained a family altar this week?
2. How well are you able to spend significant daily time with each member of your immediate family? Is your vocation taking too much time away from this priority?
3. Have you had a date with your spouse and children this week?
4. Are you spending the time and energy it takes to "disciple" your child? Your spouse?
5. Are there any unresolved conflicts or issues that you need to talk over with your spouse or children?
6. Have you made any special gestures or gifts of time or effort for your spouse? Each of your children?
7. What are your biggest struggles in this area of your life? Your biggest victories?

Chapter 8 Bible Study/Resource Suggestions

Below are suggestions for individuals and small groups who would like to study daily Christian living further. Members of a small group may study some of the Scripture passages prior to the group meeting and share their insights upon convening. Two methods of Bible study are described in Appendix E.

Time Study Passages/Questions:
Psalm 90 What are the implications here for our transient earthly lives, in light of God's eternity?

Mark 6:30-32 This passage follows the disciples' first foray into ministry. What does it have to say about the use of time?

Acts 2:46-47 What was the priority of the early Christians?

Ephesians 5:15-16 How can we apply Paul's admonition in our daily living? Compare Colossians 4:5.

Relationships Study Passages/Questions:
Matthew 5:21-26 How does Jesus extend the Mosaic Law? What is His emphasis? Why are murder and anger equated?

Luke 19:1-10 What implications did Zaccheus' salvation have for his business and social relationships?

John 13:34-35 What is the hallmark of a Christian disciple?

1 Corinthians 6:1-8 How does Paul counsel us to resolve disputes among believers? Why is our handling of conflict important?

1 Corinthians 13 Which aspects of love, as described in this passage, do you find most difficult to express in your relationships with others?

Galatians 6:1-5 What guidelines does Paul give for Christian relationships? What commands do you see? What warnings?

Ephesians 4:22-32   What actions should characterize the "new self"? How many of them are relational in nature?

James 3   What quality of the tongue does each of Paul's analogies—bit, rudder, and fire—illustrate? Why can the tongue, with little physical power, wreak such destruction?

Attitude Study Passages/Questions:
Psalms   With the help of a concordance, trace the words "joy," "rejoice," and "praise" through a single psalm or the entire book. Note the situations in which many of the psalms were composed.

Matthew 5:10-12   How are joy and gladness possible in the midst of persecution?

Philippians 4:4-9   What attitudes does Paul urge us to exhibit? Name a practical way you can express each one.

Colossians 3:12-17   Can you list these elements of Christlikeness? From that list, what are your strengths and weaknesses?

Acts 16:25-34   How does the praise and singing of Paul and Silas reinforce their message?

1 Peter 4:12-19   What is the connection between rejoicing and suffering?

Power Study Passages/Questions:
Matthew 23:1-12   How did the Pharisees practice leadership? Contrast Jesus' definition of greatness.

Mark 9:33-37   What two paradoxes does Jesus use to describe leadership?

Mark 10:35-45   What is Jesus' perception of leadership? In what ways does He personify that ideal?

Luke 14:1-14   What principle about the use of power do you

see in this passage? How did it upset the conventional way of doing things in the first century? Twentieth century?

Luke 22:24-30   According to Jesus, what are the qualifications for leadership?

Acts 1:1-8   What kind of power were the disciples expecting? What did Jesus promise instead? What was the purpose of the power?

Romans 12:3-8   How are we to regard ourselves? What is the reason for our importance?

1 Corinthians 12:12-26   How is each part of the body to be treated? What does this analogy say about power?

James 2:1-13   How does James regard favoritism? Whom do you tend to show favoritism toward? Discrimination against?

Issues Study Passages/Questions:
Acts 15:1-35   What was the divisive issue in the early church? What principles for handling such conflict do you derive from this passage?

1 Corinthians 10:12-13   What is your greatest temptation to sin? How does God promise to help?

James 1:2-8   In what ways can trials be considered joy? What does confronting the difficult issues in life accomplish?

James 5:13-20   What response to difficulty does James counsel? How can you apply it to the issues at hand in your own life?

Goals Study Passages/Questions:
Genesis 1:26-28   What were God's purposes for Adam and Eve?

Genesis 6:8-9; 9:1-2   How does God's description of, and commission to, Noah compare with Genesis 1?

Genesis 17:1-8 What was God's design for Abraham? Compare with Adam and Eve, and Noah.

Matthew 28:18-20 What goal did Jesus give His disciples? How do your present goals — career, financial, and personal — reflect a commitment to this commission?

Acts 13:1-3 How were Paul and Silas' plans decided?

General Resources to Consider:
A Serious Call to a Devout and Holy Life by William Law
The Way by E. Stanley Jones
Loving God by Charles Colson
My Utmost for His Highest by Oswald Chambers
Mere Christianity and *The Screwtape Letters* by C.S. Lewis
The Pursuit of God by A.W. Tozer
A Plain Account of Christian Perfection by John Wesley

Accountability Inventory

Daily Christian Living

Time
   1. Are there any "time stealers" in your life that you need to address?
   2. Do you need to make any adjustments to assure more time for personal devotion? For your family? For your church or ministry? For yourself?

Relationships
   3. Is there anybody against whom you are holding a grudge? Do unresolved conflicts need to be resolved? Are you "out of harmony" with anybody?
   4. Is there anyone with whom you need to seek restitution?
   5. Has your speech and conversation been free of a critical and judgmental attitude? Free from gossip? Foul language and coarse joking?

Attitudes
6. How are you feeling about your life this week? Pains? Joys? Excited? Anxious? Afraid? Angry? What word would you choose to describe yourself this week?
7. Has how you have felt lately been reflected (for good or ill) in the way you've acted this week? Are adjustments needed?
8. Are you approaching life with an attitude of thanksgiving? Of joy? Of praise?
9. Have you examined your life to see if there are any annoying mannerisms, practices, or attitudes which bother other people?

Power
10. Do you have any impure ambition?
11. Have you abused your power in relationships since we last met? How so?
12. Have you shown favoritism toward the rich or powerful since we last met? How so?
13. Have you been envious of anyone?
14. Have you unduly promoted yourself since we last met?
15. What are your biggest struggles in this area of your life? Your biggest victories?
16. How can this group help you in this area of power in your life?

The Bottom Line
17. What special lesson(s) does the Lord seem to be teaching you right now?
18. Is there a continual openness to the Holy Spirit's leading, guiding, and infilling in your day-to-day living?
19. Is Jesus Christ Lord of every facet of your life? Is there any part of your life where you are reticent to let Him take control? Any part where He has some control, but not total reign? What are your strengths and weaknesses with regard to Christ's lordship in your life?
20. How can this group help you become a more "daily Christian"?

Accountability Inventory

The Practice of Accountability

Issues

1. What major issues in your life are you facing right now?

2. What do you think the Lord is trying to say to you through this/these issue(s)?

3. What needs to be done to help you confront the issue(s) and come to a satisfactory outcome?

4. What are the biggest struggles you are currently facing? The biggest recent victory?

Wesley Tracy's adapted Wesleyan Band Meeting Questions

1. Have you had any spiritual failures recently? Have you been disappointed with yourself lately, spiritually speaking? How can we be most helpful in restoring or supporting you? When we pray for and with you today, at what point should we focus our prayers?

2. What temptations or spiritual problems have you been battling lately? At what points in your life do you feel most vulnerable? Most weak right now? Most under pressure?

3. If you have been delivered from any temptations lately, would you share with us how the victory was won? Would you share with us how you have endured and survived recent trials?

4. Has the Lord revealed anything to you about your heart and life that makes you want to take a prayerful second look at your attitudes, lifestyle, service, or motivations?

5. Is there a spiritual problem so deep or so personal that you have never been able to talk to anyone about it? Can you even talk with God about it? Are you carrying excess

baggage from the past that still today keeps you defeated and depressed? Would you like to share it with us, your spiritual partners? Or, at least let us pray for you about it—would you set a time each day (or this week) when you are going to pray about this matter so we can at that very same hour pray for you wherever you are?

Appendix C

Discipleship Covenant

(adapted from Serendipity Training Manual)

1. At the end of this discipleship group the participants will be able to:

√

√

√

2. We will meet every week until _____, after which the group will be evaluated before continuing or terminating.

   We will meet on _____ (day) from _____ (time) to _____, and strive to start and close on time.

   We will meet at _____ (location).

3. We will agree to one or more of the following group disciplines:

   ____ Attendance: To give top priority to the group meetings.

   ____ Participation: To share responsibility for the group in all its activities and to demonstrate increased vulnerability.

   ____ Confidentiality: To keep anything said in the group strictly confidential.

   ____ Accountability: To give permission to group members to hold each other accountable to the goals you set for yourself.

   ____ Accessibility: To give one another the right to call upon one another in time of need—at any time of day or night.

4. Typical Group Agenda and Time Balance:

_____Sharing   _____Study   _____Eating

_____Prayer   _____Singing

5. Basic method used for accountability . . .

6. I agree to the following individual disciplines:

_____ Daily Prayer. Time to be spent _____

_____ Daily Scripture Study. Time to be spent/

Amount to be read _____

_____ _____

_____ _____

_____ _____

WE AGREE TOGETHER TO HONOR THIS
COVENANT_____(Signature)

_____

_____

_____

(This covenant may be reproduced for use in a small group.)

Appendix D

ACTION STEPS
Group Accountability Sheet

A truth is not learned until I am committed to a course of action that involves me in that truth. — Don Fields

Name	Specific Action	Timetable

(This sheet may be reproduced for use in a small group.)

Appendix E

BIBLE STUDY METHODS

Sample Method 1:

Observe: What does the passage say? Can I state it in my own words? Can I outline it? Apply some important questions ... who, what, when, where, how, why?

Interpret: What ...
1. principles can I find in the passage?
2. commandments do I find?
3. promises are in the passage?
4. characteristics (positive and/or negative) can be seen in the situations/people?
5. deeper significance and meaning can be found? Why does God include these principles, commands, promises, characteristics?

Apply: How do the principles apply to me?
How can I obey the commands?
How can the promises be claimed? What do I have to do?
How can I imitate/avoid the positive/negative characteristics?
What is the meaning of the Holy Words for me, my family, my church, my nation? What do I need to do?

Sample Method 2:

"ABC": A ... Analysis—rewrite/rephrase the verse(s) in my own words, outline it, pick out things like important verbs if it helps.

B ... Best verse/phrase—pick out the word(s) that mean the most to me.

C ... Covenant—write out an agreement with God about something I will do because of what I have seen in the passage.

Notes

Chapter 1

1. Jack N. Sparks, ed., *The Apostolic Fathers* (Nashville, Tenn.: Thomas Nelson, 1978), 312, 317.
2. Eberhard Arnold, ed., *The Early Christians*, "Against Celsus" (Grand Rapids, Mich.: Baker Book House, 1979), 323.
3. Ibid., 323–24.
4. John Wesley, *Wesley's Works* (Peabody, Mass.: Reprinted 1984 by Hendrickson Publishers, Inc.), vol. 5, 187.
5. Eduard Schweizer, *Church Order in the New Testament* (London: SCM Press, 1961), 227.
6. Tom Sine, *The Mustard Seed Conspiracy* (Waco, Texas: Word Books, 1981), 77.
7. Lloyd C. Douglas, *The Robe* (Boston: Houghton, Mifflin, 1942), 302.
8. A.W. Tozer, *The Pursuit of God* (Harrisburg, Pa.: Christian Publications, 1948), 17.
9. Keith Drury, *How to Establish Accountability* (self-published). Copies can be purchased from Drury who currently teaches at Indiana Wesleyan University in Marion, Indiana.
10. Archibald D. Hart, *Leadership* (Spring 1988), 28.

Chapter 2

1. Martin Luther, "Treatise on Good Works," *Works of Martin Luther*, vol. 1, 225–31.
2. Charlie Shedd, *The Exciting Church Where People Really Pray* (Waco, Texas: Word Books, 1980), 11.
3. E. Stanley Jones, *How to Pray* (Nashville: Abingdon, 1979), 3.
4. J.C. Ryle, *A Call to Prayer* (Grand Rapids: Baker Book House, 1976), 14–15.
5. E. Stanley Jones, *The Way* (Garden City, N.Y.: Doubleday and Company, 1978), 216.
6. Dick Eastman, *The Hour That Changes the World* (Grand Rapids: Baker Book House, 1978).
7. Chuck Yeager, *Yeager* (New York: Bantam, 1985), 185.
8. C.S. Lewis, *Letters to Malcolm: Chiefly on Prayer* (New York: Harcourt Brace Jovanovich, 1973), 46.

9. Brother Lawrence, *The Practice of the Presence of God* (Old Tappan, N.J.: Fleming H. Revell, 1969), 8.
10. Ibid., 17.
11. Albert Einstein, *Ideas and Opinions* (New York: Bonanza Books, 1954), 64–65.
12. Guy R. Lefrancois, *Psychology for Teaching, Fifth Edition* (Belmont, Calif.: Wadsworth Publishing Company, 1985), 49.
13. Clyde S. Kilby, ed. *An Anthology of C.S. Lewis: A Mind Awake* (New York and London: Harcourt Brace Jovanovich, 1980), 98.

Chapter 3
1. E. Stanley Jones, *Christ of the Round Table* (London: Hodder and Stoughton, 1928), 96.
2. Edythe Draper, ed., *The Almanac of the Christian World* (Wheaton, Ill.: Tyndale House Publishers, 1990), 310.
3. Charles Colson, *The Role of the Church in Society* (Wheaton, Ill., Victor Books, 1986), 18–19.
4. Win Arn, *The Pastor's Manual for Effective Ministry* (Monrovia, Calif.: Church Growth, Inc., 1990), 18, and Robert Orr in a National Seminar Series entitled, "How to Diagnose and Renew Your Church," sponsored by Church Growth, Inc.
5. Frank R. Tillapaugh, *Unleashing the Church* (Ventura, Calif.: Regal Books, 1982), 8.
6. Ibid., 16.
7. Win Arn, *The Pastor's Manual*, 18.
8. Tony Campolo, Jr., *The Success Fantasy* (Wheaton, Ill.: Victor Books, 1980), 144.
9. James Fowler, *Becoming Adult, Becoming Christian: Adult Development and Christian Faith* (New York: Harper and Row, 1984), 93.
10. Tom Sine, *Why Settle for More and Miss the Best?* (Waco, Texas: Word, 1981), 136–37.

Chapter 4
1. Ron Blue, quoted in *Discipleship Journal*, Issue 53, 1989, 24.
2. Ron Blue, *Money Matters for Parents and Their Kids* (Nashville: Thomas Nelson Publishers, 1988), 17.
3. Doris Janzen Longacre, *Living More With Less* (Scottdale,

Pa.: Herald Press, 1980), 78.

4. Howard I. Dayton, quoted in *Leadership* (Spring 1981), 62.

5. Richard Foster, *Freedom of Simplicity* (San Francisco: Harper and Row, 1981), 19.

6. Ron Sider, *Rich Christians in an Age of Hunger* (Downers Grove, Ill.: InterVarsity Press, 1979), 89.

7. Also Ex. 23:16; 34:22; Lev. 19:23-25; Num. 15:20-21; Deut. 18:4; 2 Chron. 31:5.

8. Larry Burkett, *Answers to Your Family's Financial Questions* (Pomona, Calif.: Focus on the Family Publishing, 1987), 108.

9. Ibid., 113–14.

10. Richard Foster, *Money, Sex, and Power* (San Francisco: Harper and Row, 1985), 19.

11. Ibid., 62.

12. Ron Sider, *Rich Christians*, 125.

13. Larry Burkett, *Answers*, 30.

14. Ron Sider, *Rich Christians*, 172, 174.

15. Richard Foster, *Freedom of Simplicity* (San Francisco: Harper and Row, 1981), 50.

16. John Wesley, *Wesley's Works* (Peabody, Mass.: Hendrickson Publishers, 1984), 21.

17. Charles Edward White, "What Wesley Practiced and Preached about Money," *Leadership* (Winter 1987), 27–29. Much of the previous discussion and data for the chart is an adaptation of White's discussion of Wesley.

18. John Wesley, *Wesley's 52 Standard Sermons* (Salem, Ohio: Schmul Publishing, 1967 reprint), 500.

19. Ibid.

20. J. Wesley Bready, *England Before and After Wesley* (London: Hodder and Stoughton, 1939), 238.

Chapter 5

1. E. Stanley Jones, *Abundant Living* (New York and Nashville: Abingdon-Cokesbury Press, 1942), 129.

2. Marvin R. Wilson, *Our Father Abraham* (Grand Rapids: Eerdmans, 1989), 142.

3. "A Talk with the MacDonalds," *Christianity Today*, 10 July 1987, 38.

4. "Gordon MacDonald Leaves the Helm of InterVarsity," *Christianity Today,* 10 July 1987, 38.
5. Tim Stafford, *The Sexual Christian* (Wheaton, Ill.: Victor Books, 1989), 142.
6. Ibid., 114.
7. Ibid., 115.
8. Ibid., 52.
9. James Dobson, *Love for a Lifetime* (Portland, Ore.: Multnomah Press, 1987), 89–92.
10. Ibid., 93.
11. Howard and Jeanne Hendricks, eds., *Husbands and Wives* (Wheaton, Ill.: Victor Books, 1988), 301.
12. Donald Joy, *Unfinished Business* (Wheaton, Ill.: Victor Books, 1989), 154–55.
13. Bill Hybels, *Christians in a Sex-Crazed Culture* (Wheaton, Ill.: Victor Books, 1989), 64.
14. Ibid., 36.

Chapter 6
1. Marvin R. Wilson, *Our Father Abraham* (Grand Rapids: Wm. B. Eerdmans Publishing, 1989), 174–75.
2. Ibid.
3. Clarence Jordan, *The Cotton Patch Version of Paul's Epistles* (New York: Association Press, 1968), 61.
4. John Pollock, *The Apostle: A Life of Paul* (Garden City, N.Y.: Doubleday and Co., Inc., 1960), 35.
5. Quoted in Frank Bateman Stanger's *God's Healing Community* (Nashville: Abingdon, 1978), 59.
6. "The Shape of the Nation," *U.S. News and World Report,* 7 Oct. 1985, 60–61.
7. Kenneth H. Cooper, *The Aerobics Program for Total Well-Being* (New York: Bantam Books), 115.
8. "Smart Ways to Shape Up," *U.S. News and World Report,* 18 July 1988, 46.
9. Cooper, 71.
10. Ibid., 67–68.
11. "Diet and exercise can override a genetic tendency to obesity," *Chicago Tribune,* reprinted in the *Jackson Clarion-Ledger,* 3 June 1990.

Chapter 7

1. Bob Larson, *Larson's Book of Family Issues* (Wheaton, Ill., Tyndale House Publishers, 1986), 164.
2. John Q. Baucom, *Bonding and Breaking Free* (Grand Rapids: Zondervan Publishing House, 1988), 18.
3. John Rosemond, *John Rosemond's Six-Point Plan for Raising Happy Healthy Children* (Kansas City, Mo.: Andrews and McNeel, 1989).
4. Jay Kesler, Ron Beers, and LaVonne Neff, eds., *Parents and Children* (Wheaton, Ill.: Victor Books, 1987), 57.
5. Both quotes used by Dean Merrill in *Husbands and Wives,* Howard and Jeanne Hendricks, eds. (Wheaton, Ill.: Victor Books, 1988), 271.
6. The following research is cited in *The Language of Love,* Gary Smalley and John Trent (Pomona, Calif.: Focus on the Family Publishing, 1988), 33.
7. James Dobson, *Dr. Dobson Answers Your Questions* (Waco, Texas: Word Books, 1982), 75–76.
8. John Q. Baucom, *Bonding and Breaking Free,* 138–39.
9. Merton P. and A. Irene Strommen, *Five Cries of Parents* (New York: Harper and Row Publishers, 1985), 72.
10. Spencer Marsh, *God, Man and Archie Bunker* (New York: Harper and Row Publishers, 1976), 93.
11. Neil Postman, *Amusing Ourselves to Death* (New York: Elisabeth Sifton Books, Viking, 1985), vii–viii.

Chapter 8

1. Larry King, with Peter Occhiogrosso, *Tell Me More* (New York: G.P. Putnam's Sons, 1990), 70.
2. John Wesley, *Wesley's 52 Standard Sermons* (Salem, Ohio: Schmul Publishing Co., 1982), 1954.

Chapter 9

1. Karl Menninger, *Whatever Became of Sin?* (New York: Hawthorn Books, 1973).
2. Ibid., 25.
3. Ibid., 25–27.
4. John Wesley, *Wesley's Works* (Peabody, Mass.: Hendrickson Publishers, 1984), vol. 8, 272–73.
5. Ibid.

6. Wesley Tracy, *Herald of Holiness,* February 1991, 28.

7. Gordon Cosby, *Handbook for Missions Groups* (Waco, Texas: Word Books, 1975), 140–41.

8. David Lowes Watson, *Accountable Discipleship* (Nashville: Discipleship Resources, 1986).

9. Walk to Emmaus may be contacted at P.O. Box 189, Nashville, TN 37202 (615) 340-7227.

10. Elizabeth O'Connor, *Call to Commitment* (San Francisco: Harper and Row, 1963), 34–35.

11. Edythe Draper, ed., *The Almanac of the Christian World — 1991–92 Edition* (Wheaton, Ill.: Tyndale House Publishers, 1990), 18.